Free Market Economics

A Critical Appraisal

Second Edition

ANDREW SCHOTTER

Basil Blackwell

First edition published by St. Martin's Press 1985
Second edition published by Basil Blackwell 1990

Basil Blackwell, Inc.
3 Cambridge Center
Cambridge, Massachusetts 02142, USA

Basil Blackwell Ltd
108 Cowley Road, Oxford, OX4 1JF, UK

Library of Congress Cataloging in Publication Data
Schotter, A.
    Free market economics: a critical appraisal /Andrew
    Schotter. — 2nd ed.
    p. cm.
    Includes bibliographical references.
    ✕ ISBN 1–55786–074–2. — ISBN 1–55786–066–1 (pbk.)
    1. Free enterprise. I. Title
HB95.S36 1990   89–18489
330.15′3—dc20   CIP

British Library Cataloguing in Publication Data
A CIP catalogue record for this book is available from the
British Library.

Typeset in 10 on 12pt Century Old Style
by TecSet Ltd, Wallington, Surrey
Printed in Great Britain by Billing & Sons Ltd, Worcester

Contents

Preface to Second Edition

In the eight years since I started thinking about writing this book it might have appeared as if the free market system was not in need of criticism but of emulation. The political and economic changes in the Soviet Union, Eastern Europe, and China (the events of June 1989 notwithstanding) are the obvious cases in point. The apparent triumph of free market ideas and the total discrediting of old-style socialism is an apparent vindication of the market and all those who admire it. To my mind, however, the events of the recent past make it all the more important that we take a close look at free markets; if we do not, we may blindly embrace aspects of them that are best kept at arm's length. While marveling at the successes of the free market system, we must also be cognizant of its failures and attempt to avoid them, all the more so in the cases of Eastern Bloc countries and countries like the Soviet Union and China, which are purposefully embarking on a new economic institutional journey. For them a map outlining the traps along the way might be useful. This book attempts to offer such a map and hopes to point out that, while the free market system has a great many benefits, it also has its shortcomings. To be aware of these shortcomings is not to discredit the system, but merely to recognize that it is not perfect.

During these same eight years there has been a growing perception, at least among urban Americans, that all is not well in the United

States. The increases in crime, homelessness, poverty, and water and air pollution have all led to a growing sense of despair. While big-government solutions may have become the object of ridicule, it certainly cannot be argued that the the laissez-faire policies of the past eight years have done much to alleviate these problems. Blind adherence to an ideology of the free market, untempered by any qualifications, like blind adherence to any ideology, can never form the basis of a rational public policy. This book tries to point out the qualifications that must be made to the conventional libertarian free market argument in order to make it relevant to the 1990s and beyond. In fact, it is striking that the free market arguments used by our more conservative politicians and academicians have changed little over time. While they were refreshing to many in the early Reagan years, they are beginning to sound trite and hollow today. If the argument fails to change, its popularity is bound to decline. A prime example of the staleness of the free market argument can be seen in President Bush's veto of the minimum wage law in 1989. As we see in chapter 5, the minimum wage has been a thorn in the side of conservatives for many years and the early arguments against it are still being put forth in a knee-jerk manner by contemporary politicians. However, in an era of crack dealers, this issue is much more complex and, instead of arguing for the elimination of the minimum wage, one could make a rational argument for dramatically increasing it, even with a government subsidy.

In short, free marketeers have fallen into the trap over the years of arguing that free markets are good because centrally controlled markets are bad. Hence, in an era where centrally controlled economies in other countries are disintegrating, one may be lulled into thinking that therefore unrestricted free markets are unequivocally good. My point here is that the benefits of free markets have nothing to do with the drawbacks of controlled markets—they can and should be examined in isolation.

The second edition of this book differs from the first by the addition of a new chapter on experimental economics. As stated in the new chapter 6, there has been a recent explosion of interest within the economics profession, in the area of experimental economics. Experimental economists run controlled laboratory experiments in an effort to discover the properties of economic institutions and theories. While the aim of experimental economics is not to test the properties of the free market argument, if one is selective one can find a number of articles that directly or indirectly shed some light on the descriptive validity of the assumptions that form the foundation of the argument. In chapter 6 I present a number of articles that question some of the assumptions that are dear to the heart of many free marketeers. From these articles I think we can gain a healthy skepticism which, I hope, will allow us to be more objective in evaluating the benefits of free market solutions to our social problems.

Preface to First Edition

From listening to my students and to people at cocktail parties talk about the free market system, I have come to realize that there is a great deal of misunderstanding about the free market argument. The world seems divided between people who see markets as the cure for all our problems and people who see markets as the cause of all problems.

This book takes the view that the truth lies somewhere in between. In it I attempt to apply the free market argument to a wide variety of social issues and, in doing so, to point out some of its contradictions. However, my aim is not so much to discount free market economics as to raise doubts about its validity as a solution for all social problems. The criticisms I present are immanent; that is, they do not challenge the assumptions upon which the free market argument is based but rather accept them and use them to demonstrate how they can lead to social outcomes unacceptable to a consistent free market advocate. I conclude that while markets do work in many situations, they are not panaceas, and for some problems non-market institutions may be preferable. These institutions should be organized and coordinated by the state because private incentives fail to create and control them.

This book is addressed to many audiences. First, it has been written as a supplement to the textbooks used in a number of economics courses taught at universities. Any course that uses competitive (free market) economics as its theoretical foundation would benefit from devoting time to the ideas presented here. Such courses include not only economic principles (both micro and macro) but also intermediate micro-economics and industrial organization. Other courses where this book may be useful are economics of public policy, welfare economics, and business school courses on the nature of the competitive process. Students—and, for that matter, professors—should be forced to stop and think about the subtleties of the economic arguments they use to buttress their classroom discussion and policy analysis. Few books are available that do this in a logical, non-polemical way, using modern economic ideas. This is what I attempt here.

In addition, I hope that this book will be read by intelligent laymen, policy makers, and political leaders willing to follow a logically rigorous, but generally non-mathematical, argument to its conclusion. I feel that the current social debate treats the theory of free markets in much too cavalier a manner, invoking it to justify policies without proving that such an invocation is appropriate. If there were a better understanding of the limitations of the free market argument, a more rational public policy debate might follow.

This book progresses from the general to the specific. In chapter 1, I describe the "free market economic argument," spelling out its basic assumptions and tracing their roots in the history of economic thought. Chapter 2 presents conventional criticisms of the argument, which, since few of them are immanent, are not pursued in the remainder of the book. In chapter 3 I give examples to demonstrate the benefit of organizing society along free market lines. Chapter 4 aims at pinpointing where the free market system can break down, showing how individual rationality—the cornerstone of the free market argument—is responsible for many of the system's failures. As an illustration, I review some new and some traditional instances of markets that fail to determine optimal social outcomes, reviewing work on markets with what are known as informational asymmetries, externalities, and public goods. Here the selfish individual rationality of the agents in the market destroys its results instead of leading, "as if by an invisible hand," to socially desirable outcomes. Chapter 5 then shifts us from the realm of theory to that of policy. It investigates such public-policy issues as crime, minimum wages, affirmative action, anti-discrimination laws, and educational vouchers. Chapter 6 presents a theory of justice that should be acceptable to people who subscribe to the free market ideals spelled out in chapter 1, but that may lead to outcomes that they would find undesirable. Chapter 7 looks at the most recent and the strongest assumption of rationality used in the free market argument—the assumption of rational expectations—and points out potential logical difficulties with it that, if true, would dramatically alter many of the recent macro-economic policy conclusions reached by the leaders of the rational expectations school. Chapter 8 offers reasons for the endurance of the free market system in America. Chapter 9 summarizes the discussion and offers conclusions. I hope that by the time the reader reaches this point, he will have gained a more detached and objective view of the pros and cons of free market economics.

Because there are many potential audiences for this book, there are many ways to read it. General readers interested in a quick overview of the book's argument should read chapters 1, 3, 4, 5, and 9. Professors planning to assign the book, however, should use a more sophisticated strategy geared to the course being taught and the background of the students. Chapters 3, 8, and 9 are the least difficult and require no background in economics. Chapters 1, 2, 4, 5, and 6 require exposure to introductory economics—for example, through the economic principles course. Chapter 7 calls for an intermediate amount of knowledge of economics and related disciplines. This chapter is by far the most difficult in the book and should only be assigned in more advanced undergraduate or beginning graduate courses. As for the material presented in the other chapters, however, I believe that any diligent undergraduate should have no difficulty in understanding it. Chapters 1, 2, and 3 should be read by all students, regardless of the course in which they are enrolled, while the other chapters can be selected according to the emphasis of a specific course. Except for Chapter 7, this book uses no mathematics whatsoever. Nevertheless, the analysis is still logically rigorous and possibly demanding at points. I have made it so in order to give beginning students something to strive for, while at the same time not insulting more advanced students.

When an earlier version of this book, entitled "Capitalism and Corner Solutions: Some Problems with the Conservative Argument," was circulated among my friends and colleagues at New York University, they made me realize that what I was discussing in that

somewhat polemical manuscript was not the conservative argument—which has distinct political, philosophical, and even religious
overtones—but rather the more libertarian free market argument.
Hence, I wish to thank Jess Benhabib, Clive Bull, Ray Canterbery,
Roman Frydman, Lewis Kornhauser, Janusz Ordover, Peter Rappo-
port, Mark Schankerman, and Bernard Wasow for the frankness of
their comments on that manuscript, a frankness that led me to make
drastic changes in this book over the past two years. I would yet again
like to thank Clive Bull and Lewis Kornhauser for their comments
on selected chapters of the final manuscript. I want to acknowledge
my debt to the work of Roman Frydman and Gerald O'Driscoll in the
discussion of Newcomb's problem in chapter 7. Also, I wish to thank
my editor, Michael Weber of St. Martin's Press, for his encourage-
ment and patience and for providing me with some excellent (anony-
mous) referee reports that made my revisions easier. As with all of
my work, this book was made possible in part by the support of the
Office of Naval Research, Contract No. N00 14–78–C–0598. This
support is gratefully acknowledged. Finally, I thank my wife, Anne
Howland Schotter, for her careful stylistic editing.

Andrew Schotter

1

The Free Market Argument

It is important to point out at the beginning that what I call the "free market argument" differs from what has come to be known as the "conservative argument." This is because the latter is a composite of moral, economic, and political arguments that present a multi-faceted perspective on social issues. George Nash in *The Conservative Intellectual Movement in America Since 1945* divides conservatives into three groups—the "libertarians" or classical liberals, the "traditionalists," and the "evangelical anti-communists." He claims that a full characterization of the conservative argument must take all of these groups into account. My characterization of the free market argument is closest to the libertarian view, concentrating on the classical liberal value of individual rights and avoiding the emotional and moralistic concerns of the "traditionalists" and "evangelical anti-communists." I will separate the free market argument from the conservative argument and investigate it in isolation.

THE CHARACTERISTICS OF THE ARGUMENT

The free market argument is characterized by several attributes, not all of which are logically consistent. First, it is invariably individualistic, holding that all social action must

1

be sanctioned by the will of the rational individuals composing society. Under this view society is nothing more than the aggregate of the individuals composing it. Normatively this implies that no external ethic should be applied to social decisions other than by the will of the people. Norms such as equality and equity are relevant to social debate only if invoked by all of the individuals in society. Such norms should not be imposed upon society by a government or a social planner who values them for their own sake. A concomitant of this individualistic philosophy is the Lockean idea that people have an inviolable right to keep what they have earned. According to this view, no external authority has the right to expropriate these earnings through taxes.

The free market argument assumes that economic and social agents are rational in that they are fully aware of their own preferences and capable of making all of the calculations necessary to pursue their interests efficiently. This assumption of rationality has recently been taken to extremes by the rational expectations school, whose work we will discuss in chapter 8. This assumption has two components—utility maximization and selfishness. Under the first component social and economic agents are seen to make decisions that bring them the greatest satisfaction. Under the second, social and economic agents view any social state (e.g., income distribution) in terms of their own allocation of goods without regard to the consequences that the state might have for other agents' allocations. Adam Smith claimed that nothing more than selfishness is necessary for society to achieve optimal social outcomes.

> It is not from the benevolence of the butcher, the brewer, or the baker, that we expect our dinner, but from their regard to their own interest. We address ourselves, not to their humanity but to their self-love, and never talk to them of our own necessities but of their advantages. Nobody but a beggar chooses to depend chiefly upon the benevolence of his fellow-citizens. Even a beggar does not depend upon it entirely. The charity of well-disposed people, indeed, supplies him with the whole fund of his subsistence. But though this principle ultimately provides him with all the necessaries of life which he has occasion for, it neither does

nor can provide him with them as he has occasion for them. The greater part of his occasional wants are supplied in the same manner as those of other people, by treaty, by barter, and by purchase.[1]

The selfishness assumption does not deny the possibility of socially minded behavior among rational social agents.[2] This assumption only holds that such behavior is neither a necessary nor a sufficient condition for markets to maximize social welfare.

The assumption of rationality, combined with the view that there are large numbers of economic agents, known as competitive assumption, presents the fiction of an economy composed of isolated individual agents pursuing their own self-interest without considering how their actions affect the lives of others. Such interdependencies will be seen to present problems for the workings of free markets and historically have been the basis of most of their criticism.

The free market argument is usually either utilitarian or what I shall call Paretian (after the nineteenth-century sociologist Vilfredo Pareto, who devised a well-known standard by which to judge the efficiency of social states) and efficiency-oriented in its calculations. If individualism dictates that only the preferences of individuals are allowed to count in making social decisions, then these preferences must be aggregated. For example, in a cost-benefit analysis a project's social costs and benefits are added to see if the project should be undertaken.

If a utilitarian standard is used, preference intensities (perhaps expressed in dollars) are simply added up. If a Paretian standard is used, only the alternative that is the unanimous choice of the entire society is chosen. For instance, if society must build a road through either a bird sanctuary or a suburban neighborhood, the decision should be determined by which interested group—naturalists or suburban residents—is willing to pay more to have the road's location changed. If the naturalists are willing to pay $1,000,000 to avoid the road and the suburban dwellers are willing to pay only $800,000, then it should be built in the suburbs. In being willing to pay only $800,000, the suburban dwellers in essence are admitting that they will accept the road in their neighborhood as long as a bribe of that size is offered to them. We know that the naturalists are willing to pay at least $1,000,000 for that purpose, and thus they could offer the suburbanites a sufficient bribe. Hence, building the road in the suburbs is deemed best for society, since the suburbanites can be compensated by the naturalists in such a way that both parties are better off. Notice that this calculation uses only the information of individual preference and therefore is consistent with the free market individualistic bias. No external ethic, such as "the environment should be preserved," is invoked. If the individuals involved want bird life destroyed, it should be destroyed.[3]

This problem points up an inherent tension between utilitarian and libertarian aspects of the free market argument. Building the road through the suburbs is bound to violate individual rights, especially if suburbanites have to be relocated. Consistent individualists should not be willing to do so just because of a utilitarian calculation. Rather, we should build the road there only if either *all* people agree voluntarily that it is best or they can be bribed to accept it. This is a more liberatarian or contractarian view of individualism, which we will later introduce the Pareto principle to justify.[4] In fact, this conflict is evident in the utilitarian motto "the greatest good for the greatest number." The social decision that maximizes the greatest good or the greatest sum of individual utilities may turn out to benefit a minority of the population that feels intensely about the decision under consideration. Hence we may maximize the greatest good but not for the greatest number.

The free market argument is what Robert Nozick calls a "process-oriented" argument, as opposed to an "end-state-oriented" argument.[5] Process orientation assumes that in judging the outcomes of social institutions, one should not concentrate on their ethical properties but on the institutional process through which these outcomes are determined. For example, unequal income distribution in the United States is not *prima facie* evidence that incomes should be redistributed as long as the process through which they were determined did not involve fraud or coercion and was otherwise fair. If the outcome was arrived at voluntarily by the mutual consent of all involved, it can be justified, since, given the individualistic bias of the free market argument, nothing that individuals enter into voluntarily can be bad.

Another assumption of the free market argument I call the "invisible-hand laissez-faire faith assumption." This assumption holds that if individuals are left alone and allowed to contract voluntarily, the welfare of society will be enhanced. Any intervention in this process is bound to make things worse.

The final assumption of the free market argument is the efficiency-equity tradeoff assumption. Advocates of free markets maintain that if society uses a nonindividualistic social ethic to define the equity of social outcomes, there is likely to be a dropoff in the efficiency of existing institutions. Society is forced to choose between an economic system that maximizes social output (the free market) and one that maximizes some nonindividualistic ethical objective, such as the socialist ethic of "from each according to his ability, to each according to his need" or the Rawlsian ethic of maxi-min justice.[6] The latter is named after the philosopher John Rawls, who, in his book *A Theory of Justice,* advocates an ethic according to which social decisions are made in a way to maximize the satisfaction of the worst-off person in society—the "maxi-min" criterion.

The free market argument, then, is based on the rights of the individual, uses only his preferences in making its utilitarian or Paretian calculations, and, assuming the rationality of individuals, has faith in the ability of the unbridled free enterprise system to maximize the sum of these preferences.

THE INTELLECTUAL ROOTS OF THE FREE MARKET ARGUMENT

A brief examination of the historical development of the preceding assumptions will cast light on the strengths and weaknesses of the contemporary free market argument.

Individualism

Though individualism can mean many things to many people, I will distinguish only two meanings here. In one sense used by Hayek, individualism is primarily a theory of society and of social institutions. It explains the nature, evolution, and function of such institutions in terms of the unplanned and unintended action of free individual agents.[7] This emphasis on the unplanned aspect of institutions contrasts with a study of their creation or design by some centrally controlled planner.[8] Hayek states:

> It is the contention that, by tracing the combined effects of individual actions, we discover that many of the institutions on which human achievements rest have arisen and are functioning without a designing and directing mind; that, as Adam Ferguson expressed it, "nations stumble upon establishments which are indeed the result of human action but not the result of human design;" and that the spontaneous collaboration of free men often creates things which are greater than their individual minds can fully comprehend.[9]

Individualism for Hayek is intimately connected with the invisible-hand laissez-faire faith assumption. Both beliefs sanctify individuals and trust in their ability to create spontaneously and unconsciously social institutions that further society's aims better than institutions consciously designed by the same people.[10] It is in the generation of what Hayek calls a "spontaneous order"—superior in terms of social welfare to any planned social order—that the free individual is so necessary.

I will expand on this theoretical conception of individualism later in connection with the invisible-hand laissez-faire faith assumption. A second meaning of individualism is derived from a political philosophy that looks to the individual as the ultimate reservoir for all rights and obligations in society. This view is seen clearly in John Locke's famous analysis of how the political state emerges from a "state of nature." Locke views humanity in the state of nature as totally free and endowed with its full set of natural rights.[11] The political state is created at the will of the individuals existing in the state of nature solely to maintain their rights and property. If this purpose is not served, the people have the right to revolt and change their government.

> Wherever law ends, tyranny begins, if the law be transgressed to another's harm. And whosoever in authority exceeds the power given him by the law, and makes use of the force he has under his command, to compass that upon the subject, which the law allows not, ceases in that to be a magistrate, and acting without authority, may be opposed, as any other man, who by force invades the right of another.[12]

Hence, once created, neither the state nor society has rights of its own but must be the servant of the individuals that create it.

What consequences does this Lockean notion of individualism have for social policy? It implies that the state has no right to judge or alter a social outcome determined by freely contracting individuals as long as it was reached in a manner that violated no one's rights. This is true because that outcome reflects the collective will of the individuals composing society and is the equilibrium result of the "natural order" that results from free individuals. According to Locke, individuals have the right to keep anything that they mix with their labor:

> Though the earth, and all inferior creatures be common to all men, yet every man has a property in his own person. This nobody has any right to but himself. The labor of his body, and the work of his hands, we may say, are properly his. Whatsoever then he removes out of the state that nature hath provided, and left it in, he hath mixed his labor with, and joined to it something that is his own, and thereby makes it his property.[13]

As we will see later, the notion of property rights discussed here is a central characteristic of the free market argument.

Utilitarianism and the Pareto Criterion

If the individual is to be the sanctified atom of social life from which all social molecules are constructed, then it becomes necessary to create some calculus that will permit us to know when society, defined as the aggregate of individuals, is made better or worse off by a certain policy. As Jeremy Bentham wrote,

> The happiness of the individuals of whom a community is composed, that is, their pleasure and their security, is the end and the sole end which the legislator ought to have in view: the sole standard, in conformity to which each individual ought, as far as depends upon the legislator, to be made to fashion his behavior.[14]

Such a calculus, called the "felicific calculus," was proposed by the utilitarian philosophers of the eighteenth and nineteenth centuries—Jeremy Bentham (1748–1832), James Mill (1773–1836), and John Stuart Mill (1806–1873). Although utilitarianism today is looked upon as a philosophical apology for the status quo, it was quite radical when first proposed and in fact was used by Bentham as a weapon to press for legal reforms. It opposed the more libertarian view held by Locke, Adam Smith, and other individualists that God created a natural order that generally should not be interfered with by government. For Bentham and the utilitarians, the status quo is not sacred, since government intervention to increase the happiness of society is justifiable. But how is society's happiness to be measured? Bentham answers:

> The community is a fictitious body, composed of individual persons who are considered as constituting as it was its members. The interest of the community then is what?—the sum of the interests of the several members who compose it.[15]

But this answer has been unsatisfactory to twentieth century economists, since it has not been clear to them how one *measures* the interests of an individual. The solution given by the early neoclassical economists Jevons, Edgeworth, and

Marshall was to construct a utility function for each individual that would explain the satisfaction he or she got from each good or combination of goods he consumed. Such a function was calibrated in units of satisfaction called "utils." Later the economists John Hicks and R. G. D. Allen recognized that absolute utility measurement may not be possible and offered a more relative, ordinal function. Hence the utilitarian creed, "the greatest happiness for the greatest number," means arranging the laws and institutions in society so that the sum of the utilities of individuals is maximized.

However, utilitarian calculations involve a major technical problem: they assume that the levels of satisfaction of individuals can be compared. For instance, in our earlier example of the road to be built through a bird sanctuary or a suburb, we needed an operational method of making comparisons between the utility lost by one group and that gained by the other. The method proposed was simply to build the road where the willingness to pay to have it built elsewhere was smallest—in this case in the suburbs. But if income is not "optimally" distributed and if the naturalists are rich and the suburbanites are poor, a dollar would mean less to the former than to the latter. As a result, the "cheap-utility" dollars offered as bribes by the naturalists would not be comparable to the "expensive-utility" dollars offered as bribes by the suburbanites. We would have to make interpersonal comparisons of the utility of dollars.

One way out of this impasse was offered by Vilfredo Pareto, who proposed the Pareto criterion that allows us to rank social outcomes and the decisions that determine them without making interpersonal comparisons of utility. This criterion can be illustrated with the following example. Consider a world with two people, A and B, and two commodities, apples and oranges. A loves oranges and hates apples, and B loves apples and hates oranges. We are contemplating two allocations, one in which all oranges are given to A (the orange lover) and all apples are given to B (the apple lover), and one involving the opposite allocation. Clearly we can say unambiguously that the first allocation is preferable to the second because all agents in society unanimously prefer it: the apple lover gets the apples and the orange lover gets the oranges. No interpersonal comparison of utility is needed because of this unanimity. The social state that results from a particular allocation or decision is called "Pareto optimal" if no other state is unanimously preferred to it. The outcome is efficient because of the unanimity of opinion supporting it. This criterion is the one most consistent with the individualism implicit in the free market libertarian argument. If all people prefer state 1, no one has the right to deny it to them.

While the Pareto criterion is a great advance in the treatment of such problems, it comes at a cost, since it cannot be applied to all comparisons of social states. Because the criterion can only rank those states that society can unanimously decide upon, some social states are left in an ambiguous position. To get around this problem, economists have used what is called the compensation principle.[16] According to this principle, social state X is superior to social state Y if, in moving from Y to X, the people who gain can compensate the people who lose. This criterion has several characteristics. First, it does not solve the problem of interpersonal comparison of utility, since it again forces us to compare the utility gains of gainers with the utility losses of losers.[17] Second, the compensations called for under this principle need not actually be paid—the losers may remain losers. All that is required is that the gainers be able to compensate them.

The compensation principle typically infuriates modern-day liberals because it strikes them as unfair. Consider a rent-controlled apartment building occupied by elderly people. The owner decides that, because of low rental income and high oil prices, it is no longer worthwhile to keep the building and converts it into a cooperative. Should social policy allow such an action? Supporters of the compensation principle would suggest that we ask the prospective apartment owners (the gainers) how much they would be willing to pay for their apartments. We should also ask the present occupants how much they would be willing to pay to keep their apartments (this would reflect both their income and their cost of moving elsewhere). If the price that the prospective cooperative owners are willing to pay is greater than that for the apartment's current occupants (i.e., gainers can compensate losers), the apartment house should be turned into a cooperative. The compensation principle does not require that the buyers actually pay compensation because, on individualistic grounds, society has no right to decide that the happiness of apartment dwellers is more important than that of coop owners. Such a value judgment would be tolerated in an individualistic society only if the coop owners agreed to it. Hence, the use of a compensation criterion for making social decisions is nicely complementary to the individualistic ethic of free market advocates.

The Invisible-Hand Laissez-Faire Faith Assumption

Probably the greatest contribution of Adam Smith was his insistence that the freedom of individuals to maximize their own interests leads "as if by an invisible hand to promote an end which was no part of his intention." In *The Wealth of Nations* the unintended result of an individual's work, achieved through the operation of the invisible hand, is the production of the largest possible social product of the economy. In *Theory of Moral Sentiments,* written 17 years earlier, Smith also considers the appropriate distribution of this social product:

> They are led by an invisible hand to make nearly the same distribution of the necessities of life, which would have been made, had the earth been divided into equal portions among all its inhabitants, and thus without intending it, without knowing it, advance the interests of society and afford means for the multiplication of the species.[18]

Smith's beliefs, of course, were the result more of faith than of logic, being closely connected to the eighteenth-century religious beliefs that a natural order would be preserved if man did not interfere with divine laws. This article of faith is the foundation for the modern belief in laissez-faire economics. But it is no longer simply a matter of faith. The great achievement of modern mathematical economic theory has been to formalize Adam Smith's faith into a logically consistent mathematical model of general competitive equilibrium and to prove what are known as the Fundamental Theorems of Welfare Economics.[19] They state that a perfectly competitive free market economy, satisfying certain assumptions, will determine a competitive equilibrium outcome that is Pareto optimal. In other words, given limited resources, there can be no outcome that leaves all members of society better off, or at least as well off, as the outcome of a freely competitive economy.

In recent years, F. A. Hayek has concluded that the same invisible hand that maximizes the total social product can also lead individuals to evolve a wide variety of unintended social institutions that optimize social welfare.[20] The "spontaneous order" of society that results, according to Hayek, is more likely to be consistent with individual liberty and productivity than any order that was centrally planned or controlled.

Process- and End-State Justification

A process-oriented view of social justice, such as the one found in Robert Nozick's *Anarchy, State and Utopia,* judges the fairness of social outcomes, such as income distributions, strictly in terms of the desirability of the process through which they were determined rather than the characteristics of outcomes (such as the disparity of income or accumulated wealth). According to libertarian thought, a process is desirable if it respects the property and other rights of the participating individuals and does not coerce them. Consider a world in which there are three people—person A, Joe Frazier, and Muhammad Ali. Each person receives $100. Frazier and Ali agree to box each other, charge person A $50, and split the proceeds at $30 for Ali and $20 for Frazier. Person A, an avid fight fan, agrees and happily hands over $50. At the end of the fight, the income distribution is $130 for Ali, $120 for Frazier, and $50 for person A. Although an advocate of end-state principles of justice might say that this state is unfair because income is not distributed equally, Nozick would argue quite the opposite, since these agents *voluntarily* traded away from the equal income distribution and, as a result, Ali and Frazier have a right to keep what they earned without coercion. The process justifies the outcome and not vice versa; the means justifies the end. This process orientation has led many social scientists to look upon social justice as a matter of the government designing just social institutions or establishing fair rules of social interaction. Once that is done, outcomes must be left unchanged. This view, seen clearly in Hayek's *Law, Liberty and Legislation,* has led James Buchanan, Geoffrey Brennan, and others to search for the design of optimal social constitutions to help us run our social and economic lives.

But how can we judge the fairness of social processes? The free market answer, not surprisingly, is that a fair process is one that the agents would have unanimously agreed to or contracted for if they had been in a Lockean state of nature. Since this view of social justice is probably the only one consistent with the other assumptions of the free market argument, it is not surprising that it has surfaced in the social debate surrounding such important matters as income distributions and property rights.

The Efficiency-Equity Tradeoff

The efficiency-equity tradeoff assumption is a concept that has arisen out of recent microeconomic and public-finance literature on the incentive aspects of prices and taxes. Probably one of the most striking examples of the desire of neoclassical economists to separate issues of equity from those of efficiency can be seen in Richard Musgrave's *The Theory of Public Finance,* which assigns the government three separate functions: to promote efficiency, equity, and stabilization of the economy. The policies that promote equity often contradict those that promote efficiency and stabilization, and consequently social planners must make tradeoffs when formulating policy.

Rationality and Selfishness

The idea that economic man is self-interested and rational goes back to Adam Smith, who saw the economy composed of a set of self-interested agents whose selfishness is checked by the competition of others:

> The desire of bettering our condition [is] a desire which though generally calm and dispassionate, comes with us from the womb and never leaves us until we go to the grave. In the whole interval which separates these two moments there is scarce perhaps a single instant in which any man is so perfectly and completely satisfied with his situation, as to be without any wish of alteration or improvement of any kind.[21]

Modern free market thought couples a belief in this self-interestedness with a belief that economic agents are rational calculators capable of solving the implicit mathematical maximization problems they face in their everyday lives. This view comes to us from the early microeconomists who developed the theory of utility—Dupuit, Jevons, and Menger. In order to develop the theory of demand (which was lacking in the classical economists' presentation), economists had to depict economic agents as striving to maximize their utility (through the calculus of pleasure and pain) by choosing the commodity bundle that was best for them. By equating utilities at the margin, economic man was depicted as a rational automaton whose role in life was to solve constrained maximization problems given fixed prices. Hence, rationality in economics became tied to the concept of maximization. As Jevons wrote,

> Pleasure and pain are undoubtedly the ultimate objects of the Calculus of Economics. To satisfy our wants to the utmost with the least effort—to procure the greatest amount of what is desirable at the expense of the least that is undesirable—in other words, to maximize pleasure, is the problem of Economics.[22]

This assumption of rationality and maximization gives economic theory its elegance and places it, in terms of rigor, above the other social sciences, which lack such a rationality base. However, as we will see, it is this assumption of rationality that creates a variety of problems for the free market argument that ultimately weaken it.

NOTES

1. Adam Smith, *The Wealth of Nations,* Indianapolis: Liberty Classics, 1981.
2. See Howard Margolis, *Selfishness, Altruism and Rationality: A Theory of Social Choice,* New York: Cambridge University Press, 1982.
3. See William F. Baxter, *People or Penguins: The Case for Optimal Pollution,* New York: Columbia University Press, 1974.
4. See James Buchanan, "A Contractarian Paradise for Applying Economic Theory," *American Economic Review,* 65(2), May 1975, pp. 225–231.
5. Robert Nozick, *Anarchy, State and Utopia,* New York: Basic Books, 1976.
6. See John Rawls, *A Theory of Justice,* Cambridge, MA: Harvard University Press, 1971.
7. F. A. Hayek, *Individualism and Economic Order,* Chicago: University of Chicago Press, 1948. For a view similar to Hayek's, see Andrew Schotter, *The Economic Theory of Social Institutions,* New York: Cambridge University Press, 1981.
8. This view is also presented in David Hume, *A Treatise on Human Nature,* Oxford: Oxford University Press, 1896.
9. Hayek, *Individualism,* pp. 6–7.
10. F. A. Hayek, *Law, Legislation and Liberty,* Chicago: University of Chicago Press, 1976.
11. For a modern analysis of how a "minimal state" emerges from a state of nature in a manner that preserves individual rights, see Robert Nozick, *Anarchy, State and Utopia.*
12. John Locke, *Two Essays on Government,* Cambridge, England: Cambridge University Press, 1960, pp. 418–419.
13. *Ibid.,* pp. 305–306.
14. Jeremy Bentham, *Principles of Morals and Legislation,* Oxford: Wilfred Harrison, 1948, Chapter 3, Section i.
15. *Ibid.,* Section iv.
16. N. Kaldor, "Welfare Propositions of Economics and Interpersonal Comparisons of Utility," *Economic Journal,* 49, 1939, pp. 549–552.

17. See William Baumol, *Welfare Economics and the Theory of the State,* London: Longmans Green, 1952.
18. Adam Smith, *Theory of Moral Sentiments,* Oxford: Clarendon Press, 1976.
19. See Gerard Debreu, *The Theory of Value,* New York: Wiley, 1959; and Kenneth Arrow and Frank Hahn, *General Competitive Analysis,* San Francisco: Holden Day, 1970.
20. Hayek, *Law, Legislation and Liberty.* See also Schotter, *The Economic Theory of Social Institutions.*
21. Adam Smith, *Wealth of Nations,* pp. 324–325.
22. William Jevons, *The Theory of Political Economy,* Middlesex, England: Penguin, 1970. Use of this quotation is unfortunate, because Jevons claims that individuals want the greatest pleasure at the least cost, while the true maximization problem involves maximizing the difference between pleasure and cost.

2

Standard Criticisms of the Free Market Argument

Chapter 1 discusses value judgments or assumptions upon which the free market argument is based. For instance, the argument is individualistic in that its advocates believe that the individual is the fundamental unit of the social structure. To the extent that one does not share this assumption, one is likely to disagree with free market conclusions. Likewise, one must accept the relevance and appropriateness of particular economic models before one can accept the invisible-hand laissez-faire faith assumption that social outcomes will be optimal if individuals are left free to barter and exchange. Similarly, the process orientation and belief in an equity-efficiency tradeoff are intimately related to and dependent on assumptions concerning the place of the individual in the social order and stand or fall with one's view on that issue.

In the present text I am mainly interested in making immanent criticisms of several free market arguments, which do not challenge assumptions but rather accept them and follow them to their natural conclusions. This is not to say that one must or should accept these assumptions. In fact, most standard criticisms of the free market argument attack its assumptions. To review these criticisms, I shall outline some of the standard contemporary criticisms of the free market argument.

INDIVIDUALISM

Although it seems quite natural to most Americans, the notion that the individual and not the group should be the basic repository of rights and obligations is neither old nor universally accepted. In primitive cultures there is very little sense of individual identity. Property, far from being private, is held in common and all individual rights are subservient to those of the village chief. Furthermore, goods and services are invariably allocated not by the principle of marginal productivity—that each person gets what he contributes—but by customary rules. One might argue that such societies are not efficient and have not succeeded in sustaining themselves largely because they did not generate efficient economic organizations. Societies based on the rights of individuals may well be more productive than those in which group rights dominate, but unless one assumes that the only goal of social organization is production and that questions of equity are irrelevant, one should not be disturbed by this.

However, one does not have to travel back into history or to contemporary primitive societies to find views of the individual that differ from those of modern American libertarians. In many modern societies people conduct their lives with more of a communal spirit than in the United States. In such societies it is bad form to place one's own goals ahead of those of the group. Japan is an obvious example of such a society. America has recently begun to learn the bitter lesson that it could be outperformed by a society where the group rather than the individual is supreme in the workplace and the marketplace. In *The Art of Japanese Management*, Richard Tanner Pascale and Anthony Athos point out that the key to the success of the Matsushita Electric Company, the focus of their study, is its value system. This system requires employees to commit themselves to serve society as well as to make money, and uses group decision making and a communal spirit to increase social cohesiveness (each day Matsushita employees sing the company song). The authors state that the Matsushita system combines the "rationalism of the West with, the spiritualism of the East." Thus one criticism that might be leveled against the free market argument is that it is based on an assumption of the supremacy of the individual that is historically and culturally parochial.

Another criticism of the individualistic ethic is found in Kenneth Arrow's *Individual Choice and Social Value,* which proves that social decisions based only on individual preferences cannot be rational because in general there is no consistent voting mechanism to transform individual preferences into social preferences. The common example used to demonstrate this point is the paradox of voting first presented by the eighteenth century mathematician and philosopher Condorcet.[1] Assume that a community of three people must decide among three alternatives: building a swimming pool (A), building a school (B), or building neither (C). Each individual in the town has preferences among these alternatives and is able to rank them according to which he or she prefers best, second best, and least. These preferences are as depicted in Figure 2-1. Which alternative should the community choose if

INDIVIDUALS

		1	*2*	*3*
	First	A	C	B
RANKINGS	*Second*	B	A	C
	Third	C	B	A

Figure 2–1. The paradox of voting

only the preferences of the individuals are to count in making the choice? How should this choice be made? Clearly, given the individualistic assumptions we have been describing, we would want the decision process to be non-dictatorial, since we want all people's preferences to count equally. A natural solution would be to use majority rule. But this solution poses a problem, since no matter which alternative society chooses, there will always be a majority of the population that will prefer some other alternative. If A were chosen, voters 2 and 3 would prefer C to it; if C were chosen, voters 1 and 3 would prefer B to it; and if B were chosen, voters 1 and 2 would prefer A to it. There is no optimal social decision. But this problem of cyclicity arises not only with the majority voting system but, as Arrow demonstrates, with *all* nondictatorial voting systems. Hence, even a devoted individualist could not logically require that all social decisions be made *only* on the basis of the preferences of individuals, because no voting mechanism is capable of doing this in a rational, non-dictatorial way. Social decisions will have to be made upon the basis of more information than individual preferences alone. Some external ethic must be imposed.

THE UTILITARIAN AND THE PARETIAN ETHICS

The Utilitarian Ethic

Utilitarianism has been the focus of debate among philosophers and economists for the past 150 years.[2] Recent economists have raised several criticisms of utilitarianism and utilitarian calculations. One of the most important criticisms is that these calculations rely on a knowledge of the intensity of individuals' preferences, which can be determined only by personal reports. Since individuals may intentionally report false preferences, calculations may be based on incorrect information and not be optimal in utilitarian terms. Although some impressive steps have been taken to rectify this preference revelation problem, it has created a great stumbling block in applying utilitarianism to social decisions.[3]

On a more philosophical level, utilitarianism has most often been criticized as being vulnerable to the whims of a small minority with intense feelings about a particular issue. For instance, as Amartya Sen points out, if Nero received exquisite pleasure from fiddling while Rome burned, and the losses of the inhabitants were much less intense, then by a utilitarian calculation we might reach the conclusion that the city should have been burned.[4] The huge majority may be asked to sacrifice for the utility of a tiny, but greedy minority.

Utilitarianism also does not allow society to evaluate the merits of the sources of pleasure and pain. If people prefer to use public funds to build a pornographic movie theater rather than an opera house, no utilitarian can consistently object by saying that some types of art are more worthwhile than others.[5]

Many social states that seem unjust can be justified by utilitarian calculations. For example, slavery can be deemed acceptable on utilitarian grounds if the increased happiness of the slave owner is greater than the increased pain inflicted on the slave by his captivity. Criticism of utilitarianism attacks such a consequentialist mentality,[6] which justifies acts if and only if they bring beneficial consequences.

Another criticism of utilitarianism stems from its lack of concern for distributional issues. For instance, in our example of the road, the operational definition of preference intensity used by utilitarians is the "willingness to pay" of the agents under consideration. Hence, if society is willing to pay $1,000,000 for a golf course and only $200,000 for a hot-lunch program, and both projects are equally expensive, we should have a golf course and not hot lunches. Members of society should "vote with dollars" for what they want and express their preference in their willingness to pay. But since dollars are not distributed equally, under a willingness-to-pay standard the rich would have an unfair advantage. This point is ironic, since utilitarianism can also be used to justify an equal distribution of income when tax policies are being discussed.[7]

The Paretian Ethic

In order to get around some of the problems created by the application of the utilitarian ethic to social decisions, economists have resorted to a unanimity criterion called the Paretian ethic. This ethic requires every individual in society to agree on a social decision before it can be taken.

One disturbing problem concerning the Paretian ethic for the free market argument was pointed out by Amartya Sen.[8] He discovered that choosing between social alternatives in a way that respects people's individual rights—satisfies what he calls a condition of Liberalism—and also determines outcomes that are Pareto optimal may be impossible. In other words, insisting upon Pareto-optimal outcomes may be inconsistent with a respect for individual rights.

To understand Sen's point, let us first recognize that a strict individualist might argue that there are certain social choices over which some individual should be the sole decision maker. For instance, whether I sleep on my back or stomach is my own business, and an individualist would insist that I alone should make this decision. Sen calls this attitude the condition of Liberalism. To demonstrate that such a condition may be inconsistent with society's ability to make decisions that satisfy this condition as well as satisfy Pareto optimality, consider Sen's "Paradox of the Paretian Liberal":

Let the social choice be between three alternatives involving Mr. A reading a copy of *Lady Chatterley's Lover*, Mr. B reading it, or no one reading it. We name these alternatives a, b, and c, respectively. Mr. A, the prude, prefers most that no one read it, next that he reads it, and last that "impressionable" Mr. B be exposed to it, i.e., he prefers c to a, and a to b. Mr. B, the lascivious, prefers that either of them should read it rather than neither, but further prefers that Mr. A should read it rather than he himself, for he wants Mr. A to be exposed to Lawrence's prose. Hence he prefers a to b, and b to c. A liberal argument can be made for the case that given the choice between Mr. A reading it and no one reading it, his own preference should be reflected by social preference. So that society should prefer that no one reads it, rather than having Mr. A read what he plainly regards as a dreadful book. Hence c is socially preferred to a. Similarly, a liberal argument exists in favor of reflecting Mr. B's preference in the social choice between Mr. B reading it and no one reading it. Thus b is preferred to c. Hence society should prefer Mr. B reading it to no one reading it, and the latter to Mr. A reading it. However, Mr. B reading it is Pareto-worse than Mr. A reading it, even in terms of the weak Pareto criterion, and if social preference honors that ranking, then a is preferred to b. Hence every alternative can be seen to be worse than some other. And there is thus no best alternative in this set and there is no optimal choice.[9]

Consequently, if a society of individualists or classical liberals is to make group rational social choices and make them consistently, it must drop either its insistence on Pareto optimality or its insistence on liberalism.

This is not the only problem with the Paretian ethic. Consider a society that has a problem of efficiently organizing production and distributing goods. Each hypothetical organizational design determines a different configuration of incomes for the agents in society. In a world in which there are two people, the set of income distributions can be depicted as in Figure 2–2. No matter how production is organized one of

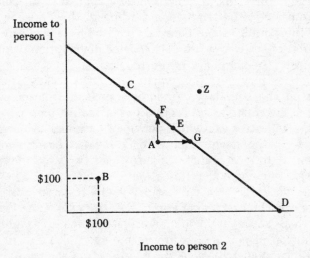

Figure 2–2. Income distributions in a two-person world

the points in the large triangle (representing a distribution of income) will result. A point, such as z, that is outside of the triangle is simply not feasible. Hence, if point B is reached, both people will receive $100. The question for economists and politicians to settle is which point within the triangle or on its boundary is desirable and how we should go about realizing it. Actually, advocates of free markets following the process-oriented approach would object to phrasing the problem this way, since they would say that we should just design a fair set of rules for economic organization regardless of the result—"let the chips fall where they may." We should not first choose the outcome we want and then design society to achieve it.

The Paretian ethic says that if we organize the institutions and regulations of society, such as legal systems and tax laws, in such a way that a point such as A is achieved, then the rules that defined that outcome should be changed since there exists another organizational plan (a different set of taxes and laws) that could yield a point such as E (or any point between F and G) that makes *all people* better off than they are at A—i.e., points E, F, and G are "Pareto superior" to point A. Since this argument can be applied to all points in the interior of the triangle, according to the Paretian ethic, only the points in the boundary can be justified. Any organization of society yielding an income distribution defined by a point on the boundary is "Pareto optimal."

Notice, however, that when we move society from one point on the boundary to another, such as from point E to point C, by changing its regulations or institutions, person 1's income is increased while person 2's income is decreased. Therefore, the move from E to C will not be *unanimously* agreed to and we cannot compare these two ways of organizing society using a Paretian ethic.

In short, the free market argument rests on two points. These are: (1) the Fundamental Theorems of Welfare Economics, which state that a free enterprise system guarantees the generation of points that are Pareto optimal (i.e., will never yield income distributions in the interior of the triangle) and (2) the ethical belief that any point on the boundary of the feasible triangle is justifiable if it has been arrived at through a process of fair play.

This argument can be applied to the debate over socialism. As we saw, the Fundamental Theorems of Welfare Economics tell us that a free enterprise system can guarantee a Pareto-optimal income distribution (i.e., a point on the frontier of the feasible triangle). Hence, if society were organized along socialist lines, an income distribution in the interior of the triangle, such as point A, could result. But at point A *all* people would want to get together (if they were free to do so) and unanimously agree to change the economic organization of society, since a point such as E exists on the frontier of the triangle at which *all* people are better off. Therefore, using a Paretian ethic, if people were free to make any agreement they wanted, they would always opt out of socialism and agree to organize society along free market lines. Hence the argument concludes that socialism must be imposed on people; they would never voluntarily choose it for themselves.

Phrased in these terms, the Paretian argument seems hard to refute. How can one argue that people should not get what they unanimously want? One standard counterargument, applied to the socialist debate, runs as follows: The Paretian criterion is neutral with respect to distribution. In other words, any point along the boundary PP′ is as good as any other, and, adopting a libertarian political philosophy, one can make an argument for never altering any income distribution that results, no matter how unequal. Hence, consider the point D in the diagram. At this point person 2 has all the income and person 1 has none. This may result because person 2 has great athletic abilities that are valued by society, while person 1 has great talent as a ballet dancer that is not marketable. According to the Paretian arguments, this unfortunate state of affairs is still optimal and should not be altered. Socialists would reply: Consider point A. If we taxed the athlete (appropriated his earnings) and distributed it to the ballet dancer, he would not work as hard and the country's GNP would fall (i.e., we would be in the interior of the triangle). Still, they would argue, it seems fairer to be there than at point D, at which the ballet dancer is given a zero income. Socialists argue that the capitalist-socialist choice is not a choice between points A and E but rather between points A and D. When put this way, it is not clear that people would opt for point D instead of A, i.e., for capitalism over socialism. In fact, as John Rawls argues in *A Theory of Justice,* free individuals who are given only the two alternatives offered here and who make this decision behind a "veil of ignorance" (i.e., without knowing who they will be in society—the athlete or the ballet dancer) would unanimously agree to the socialist alternative. This would be the system that maximizes the happiness of the worst-off person in society.[10]

Thus the unanimity or Paretian ethic receives criticism for being too extreme in requiring unanimous agreement and too insensitive to distributional questions.

Process Orientation

According to the process-oriented view of social justice, as described in Robert Nozick's *Anarchy, State and Utopia* and F. A. Hayek's *Law, Liberty and Legislation,* the justice of the outcomes of social systems should be judged strictly in terms of the properties of the process determining them. Hence, if we take the set of babies born on a given day and look at their incomes 50 years later, any discrepancies that result are justifiable as long as none of the babies have been defrauded or coerced by any of the others or anybody else in the intervening years. If one baby has greater entrepreneurial talent than another, then the difference in their eventual incomes is justifiable on that basis. The outcomes of fair games played fairly should be left alone.

One standard criticism of this argument is that the game may not be fair. A baby born into a poor family with an absent father and a drug-addicted mother cannot seriously be considered able to compete equally with another baby born into an intact upper-middle-class family. Hence, while the race for success looks fair, one of the runner's starting lines has been moved half way to the finish line. Process-oriented arguments are biased toward the preservation of the status quo.

Another criticism of the process-oriented approach is that in effect advocates of free markets put up a smoke screen, since it is ostensibly easy to figure out outcomes under any given set of rules. Arguing about rules is essentially the same thing as arguing about outcomes. Advocates of free markets respond that it is not so easy to construct a link between rules and outcomes. To their mind, the world's events are so uncertain that one cannot predict how social policies will affect people's incomes. Consequently, the design of rules will not bias the results. As Hayek argues:

> To proceed with this task we must recall once more the fundamental fact stressed at the beginning of this study: the impossibility for anyone of knowing all the particular facts on which the overall order of the activities in a Great Society is based. It is one of the curiosities of intellectual history that, in the discussion of rules of conduct, this crucial fact has been so little considered although it alone makes the significance of rules intelligible.[11]

The counterargument holds that although we may not know the absolute effects of rules on outcomes, we do have a fairly good idea of their distributional impact—who is helped by certain rules and who is hurt. For instance, take the rule in basketball that forbids players to stand under the basket for more than three seconds. If this rule were eliminated, the incomes of tall players in the league would immediately be increased, since their effectiveness would be far greater if they could hang under the basket, block shots, and dunk the ball. (This assumes that attendance does not fall because the game becomes more boring.) Hence, the counterargument goes, if the rules of basketball were not imposed from above but set by voluntary agreement among the players, as many contractarians would desire, the debate would be about outcomes and not rules, or at least about outcomes disguised as rules. You cannot divorce the rules that society uses from the outcomes that these rules determine.

The Invisible-Hand Laissez-Faire Faith Assumption

References to Adam Smith's invisible hand can be seen everywhere in the contemporary American social debate. The idea that free individuals left alone to barter and exchange will determine an optimal social state is a basic tenet of the American belief in free enterprise. This idea has been justified in modern economic theory, which has proven that, under special circumstances, free market outcomes are indeed Pareto optimal. Adam Smith was partly right. However, in their proof of what may be called the invisible hand theorem, economists discovered that the circumstances under which this theorem is true are severely limited. For instance, there must be no externalities present in the economy. This means that the utility that each consumer gets from the goods he consumes must be independent of the utility from goods consumed by others, and that the cost of production of each firm must be independent of the production decisions of others (see chapter 3). But such externalities are quite common. For instance, if the satisfaction that I get from owning a Cadillac depends on whether any of my friends own one, a consumption externality exists.[12] If the cost of a commercial laundry that hangs its clothes outside to dry is increased by the presence of an electric utility company whose smokestack emits soot that dirties the clothes, a production externality exists. These externalities invalidate the invisible hand theorem. In these circumstances, individuals acting freely may not determine a Pareto-optimal outcome. In fact, the outcome they determine may be quite bad.

The debate over the relevance of Adam Smith's invisible hand theorem boils down to an empirical debate over whether the world is as the economists say it is. Such debates have no satisfactory solution. But even granting the economists their assumptions, some people might argue that the invisible hand theorem is weak in that it only guarantees us that the outcomes determined are Pareto optimal. As we have seen in Figure 2–2, there exist Pareto-optimal outcomes (point D) that are far from satisfactory because they provide some people with extremely low incomes. One of these outcomes may result from the laissez-faire policies of the government. In short, when Adam Smith states that the free market will define outcomes that are socially optimal, it must be specified that they are optimal only in an extremely weak sense (Pareto optimal). Once this point is established, free market policies may take on a more limited appeal.

The Equity-Efficiency Tradeoff

One supposedly sad fact of economic and political life is that there is a tradeoff between the equity of outcomes that result from an economic system and their efficiency. For instance, if you tax the rich to assist the poor, the eventual income distribution may be more equal, and hence "fairer" (if you define fairness to mean equality). But it is almost certain that total incomes will fall because the rich will not work as hard as before.

Now there are two possible criticisms of this view. The first states that equity is a necessary condition for efficiency. The second states that even if this were not true and we had to choose between them, the choice should always be for equity, since efficiency is too weak a standard to impose by itself.

To explain these arguments, let us look at a simple example. Assume that two starving people simultaneously find a cake. Each needs at least 20 percent of the cake in order to live. How are they to divide it? One way is to give all the cake to one person and none to the other. While seemingly unfair or inequitable, this is an efficient or Pareto-optimal way to split it—there is no other split that *both* people would prefer. Unfortunately, doing this guarantees that one person will die. Another way to split the cake is to give 45 percent to one person and 45 percent to another and to throw away 10 percent. This outcome is not efficient because 10 percent of the cake is wasted, yet most people would agree that it is preferable since both people are guaranteed life. In other words, just because an outcome is efficient or Pareto optimal does not mean that it is desirable. Non-optimal worlds that are equitable may be more pleasant places in which to live.

This notion runs counter to the theories of the new field of law and economics. For example, in Richard Posner's *The Economic Analysis of the Law* and *The Economics of Justice,* the objective of the law is assumed to be solely the promotion of efficiency or wealth maximization. The idea that the legal system should dispense justice is brushed aside by a utilitarian argument that if a law were inefficient (although "fair"), the losing litigants would lose more in terms of wealth than the successful litigants would gain by the judicial decisions. Hence, if these agents could meet freely and could voluntarily determine the laws under which they should live, the present losers could bribe the present gainers to write the law differently. Through compensation, all agents would benefit from a change in the law, and therefore the law should be changed. According to this argument, a jurisdiction's law will depend on its income distribution. Recently Cooter and Kornhauser have demonstrated fallacies in this argument.[13] They show that under simple assumptions the evolution in the common law will not establish the legal rule that is most efficient or wealth maximizing but that over time a variety of legal rules, some more efficient than others, will come to be used. Inefficient rules will never be weeded out of the legal system. Hence, an invisible hand argument does not seem to apply to the law. Since efficiency is not guaranteed, questions of equity seem especially appropriate.

The second argument against the equity-efficiency trade-off is that it may be bogus. An "efficiently organized" economy may define outcomes that a substantial portion of the population may consider unfair. Those people that do relatively well under the existing set of institutions may have an incentive to work hard, but those who do poorly may become discouraged and stop trying. Now, contrast this situation with an "inefficiently organized" economy that the overwhelming majority consider to be fair. If this sense of fairness increases the effort of the previously discouraged population to a point where the average effort of workers in the economy is increased, then this "inefficient" but equitable set of institutions may produce a greater output than the "efficient" economy.[14] Hence, if people think they are playing a fair economic game and this belief causes them, on average, to try harder, equitable economic institutions may turn out to be efficient as well.

Rationality and Self-Interestedness

Perhaps because it is the cornerstone of the free market argument, the assumption of rationality has come under close scrutiny by a number of economists. An early attack on the notion that economic agents are rational maximizers came from the Carnegie-Mellon School led by Herbert A. Simon. This school doubted whether economic agents can perform the complex calculations necessary to maximize their utility and posited that such agents (and the organizations they staff) merely satisfice (i.e., set reachable goals for themselves that are satisfactory rather than maximal). For instance, when faced with complex sets of problems, economic agents may rely on rules of thumb to govern their behavior rather than react to each exogenous shock as maximizing agents might. They are rational, but boundedly so.

Advocates of the free market tend to dismiss such arguments by using an evolutionary approach. If economic agents are less than rational and use rules of thumb, then those using poor or non-optimal rules of thumb will be weeded out, leaving only those whose rules of thumb are superior. Over time, then, only maximizing rules should remain so that at the equilibrium of the process, people use rules that maximize their utility.[15] Despite this argument, however, accumulating experimental evidence indicates that economic agents do not behave in a manner consistent with the hypothesis that they maximize, especially when uncertainty exists.

When the world is known with certainty, decision making is particularly simple. Say that there are three goods in the world—apples, oranges, and hamburgers—and that you like apples most, oranges second most, and hamburgers least. If, given these preferences, you were then given a choice be-

Table 2-1. Expected returns and associated probabilities for two investments

Return on Investment A	Probability	Return on Investment B	Probability
$50	5%	$50	10%
80	30	80	20
100	30	100	20
120	30	120	30
200	5	200	20

tween one apple and one hamburger, the choice would be simple: you would choose an apple. While choices in a certain world obviously need not be this simple—some can involve complicated maximization problems—the rule is always the same: make the choice that maximizes your satisfaction according to your preference. In an uncertain world, however, things are not this simple. Assume that you have $100 to invest and your stock broker offers you a choice between two $100 investments, A and B, portrayed in Table 2-1. The two investments yield the same returns but with different probabilities. Hence, these investments are not sure things but gambles or lotteries yielding prizes with stated probabilities. Which investment should a rational individual choose?

The first person who attempted to answer this question was the mathematician Pierre Simon Laplace. He reasoned as follows: Since these investments are lotteries, we should calculate the expected monetary value of each investment and then choose the one that maximizes this value. To calculate an expected monetary value, one merely multiplies each dollar return by the probability that the decision maker can expect to get that return and add up the results.

Expected monetary value of Investment A = $50(.05) + $80(.30) + $100(.30) + $120(.30) + $200(.05) = $102.5
Expected monetary value of Investment B = $50(.10) + $80(.20) + $100(.20) + $120(.30) + $200(.20) = $117

If we were to use Laplace's rule, we would choose Investment B, because it has the largest expected monetary return.

While this process seems reasonable, it turns out that it is not the process that a rational decision maker would use. To illustrate, consider the following example. A person with no insurance is told by his doctor that he will need $20,000 to have a kidney transplant. Unless he has the operation tomorrow, he will die. He has only $10,000 in the bank and has no one to lend him the remaining $10,000. As he walks down the street, a notorious gambler offers him a choice between two risky propositions, both of which cost $10,000. The propositions appear as in Table 2–2. Which proposition should he choose? If he followed Laplace's method, he would choose Proposition 1, since its expected monetary value is far greater than that of Proposition 2. But notice that no matter the result of Proposition 1, our decision maker will die. On the other hand, Proposition 2, although it has a 90 percent chance of earning nothing, provides a 10 percent chance of winning $20,000 and living. Hence, if our decision maker values his life, he should choose Proposition 2, the one with the lower expected monetary return, and not Proposition 1.

Table 2–2. Expected monetary values for two propositions in the kidney patient problem

Return on Proposition 1	Probability	Expected return
$15,000	90%	$13,500
0	10	0
	Expected monetary value =	$13,500

Return on Proposition 2	Probability	Expected return
$20,000	10%	$2,000
0	90	0
	Expected monetary value =	$2,000

Rational decision makers are out to maximize not their expected dollar gain but the expected utility that these dollars will bring them. Proposition 1, despite its high expected dollar return, guarantees that our decision maker will die tomorrow. Under these circumstances it would be impossible for him to enjoy his monetary payoff. Proposition 2 gives a 10 percent chance of life, whose rewards one assumes are great. Hence, Proposition 2 clearly yields greater expected utility and should be chosen by a rational decision maker.

Decision making in an uncertain world is a two-step process. First, one must assign utility numbers to the prizes offered by the gambles or lotteries one is offered. Then, using these utility numbers, one should choose the lottery that maximizes one's expected utility. The hypothesis that this process characterizes the thinking of a rational decision maker is called the expected utility hypothesis. In our example, since our decision maker needed $20,000 to live, we can assume that any amount of money less than that yields him zero utility. Further, we may assume that since any amount of $20,000 or above yields him life, we can assign some positive utility number to these dollars, say 1. We can see that the expected utility of Proposition 1 is 0 while the expected utility of Proposition 2 is .1.

Expected Utility of Proposition 1 =
.9(Utility of $15,000) + .1(Utility of $0) =
.9U($15,000) + .1U($0) =
.9(0) + .1(0) = 0
Expected Utility of Proposition 2 =
.1(Utility of $20,000) + .9(Utility of $0) =
.1U($20,000) + .9U($0) =
(.1 × 1) + (.9 × 0) = .1

Hence, after assigning utilities we find that Proposition 2 is really the better and should be chosen.

But where do these utility numbers come from? In the example above they are assigned arbitrarily. John Von Neumann and Oskar Morgenstern in *The Theory of Games and Economic Behavior* prove that one can perform an experiment to elicit the utility numbers of a particular kind of decision maker.

It has become evident in recent years that people do not behave as the expected utility hypothesis predicts and as a result that the rational foundation for free market economics is shaky. Consider the following generalization of the famous paradox of Allais, as described by Paul Schoemaker.[16] In Situation A, action 1A produces a certain loss of $45, and action 2A produces a .5 chance of losing $100 and a .5 chance of losing nothing. In Situation B, action 1B gives a .1 chance of losing $45 and a .9 chance of losing $10, and action 2B gives a .05 chance of losing $100 and a .95 chance of losing nothing. Most subjects prefer action 2A to 1A and action 1B to 2B.[17] However, this does not make sense. The choice of 2A over 1A implies that the utility of 2A is greater than that of 1A, or

$$U(-\$45) < .5U(-\$100) + .5U(\$0), \text{ or}$$
$$U(-\$45) < .5U(-\$100)$$

where $U(\$-45)$ defines the utility of losing $45. If subjects prefer 1B to 2B, then

$$.1U(-\$45) + .9U(\$0) > .05U(-\$100) + .95U(\$0), \text{ or}$$
$$.1U(-\$45) > .05U(-\$100)$$

In the first case subjects prefer a chance to lose $100 that is one half the chance of losing $45, while in the second they prefer the opposite. Rational maximizers would not be so inconsistent. Kahneman and Tversky call this the certainty effect, since in situation A we are dealing with a sure loss of $45, a fact that seems to weigh inordinately in people's minds. They propose a new theory called "prospect theory" to explain such apparent anomalies. Similar types of results were reported by David Grether and Charles Plott.[18]

An interesting article by Richard Thaler summarizes a number of experimental results contradicting the utility-maximizing model.[19] For instance, in economic principles courses we are taught that opportunity costs should be treated as equivalent to out-of-pocket costs. However, this turns out not always to be verifiable experimentally. For instance, consider the following examples from Thaler.

Example 1. Mr. R bought a case of good wine in the late '50s for about $5 a bottle. A few years later his wine merchant offered to buy the wine back for $100 a bottle. He refused, although he has never paid more than $35 for a bottle of wine.

Example 2. Mr. H mows his lawn. His neighbor's son would mow it for $8. He wouldn't mow his neighbor's same-sized lawn for $20.

Example 3. Two survey questions: (a) Assume you have been exposed to a disease that, if contracted, leads to a quick and painless death within a week. The probability that you have the disease is 0.001. What is the maximum amount you would be willing to pay for a cure? (b) Suppose volunteers were needed for research on the above disease. All that would be required is that you expose yourself to a 0.001 chance of contracting the disease. What is the minimum payment you would require to volunteer for this program? (You would not be allowed to purchase the cure.) The results: Many people respond to questions (a) and (b) with answers that differ by an order of magnitude of one or more! (A typical response is $200 and $10,000.)

In these example it is clear that a great many people would behave the way the agents described behaved. The reason is that people tend not to view out-of-pocket costs in the same way as they view opportunity costs. They weigh out-of-pocket costs more heavily, and this behavior runs counter to that of a rational agent.

The rationality assumption may be suspect and, if not correct, may place economic theory and the free market argument in jeopardy. For the rest of this book, however, I will assume that people are rational, for my major aim is to accept these assumptions and to present "immanent" criticisms.

NOTES

1. Marquise de Condorcet, "Essai sur l'application de l'analyse à la probabilité des decisions rendues à la pluralets de voix," Paris, 1785.
2. For a modern view of the debate, see J. J. C. Smart and Bernard Williams, *Utilitarianism: For and Against,* Cambridge, England: Cambridge University Press, 1975.
3. See Jerry Green and Jean Jacques Laffont, *Incentives in Public Decision Making,* Amsterdam: North Holland, 1979.

4. Amartya Sen, *Collective Choice and Social Welfare,* San Francisco: Holden Day, 1970.

5. In other words, if people care more about building a swimming pool than educating their children, then they should be allowed to do so. In Bentham's words, "Pushpin is as good as poetry." No external value judgment should be imposed upon society.

6. See Smart and Williams, *Utilitarianism.*

7. See Abba Lerner, *The Economics of Control,* New York: Macmillan, 1944.

8. Sen, *Collective Choice.*

9. *Ibid.,* p. 80.

10. This example does an injustice to Rawls by claiming that his argument is a justification of socialism. As far as I know, this was not his intent and my example merely applies his argument to a particular example.

11. F. A. Hayek, *Law, Legislation and Liberty,* Chicago: University of Chicago Press, 1948, p. 8.

12. See Harvey Liebenstein, "Bandwagon, Snob and Veblen Effects in the Theory of Consumer Demand," *Quarterly Journal of Economics,* vol. 64, no. 2, pp. 183–201, 1950.

13. Robert Cooter and Lewis Kornhauser, "Can Litigation Improve the Law Without the Help of Judges?" *Journal of Legal Studies,* 9, January 1980, pp. 139–165.

14. In essence this argument is similar to the idea that the fairness or perceived fairness of an economic institution may alter the X-inefficiency of the economy. See Harvey Liebenstein, "Allocative vs. X-Efficiency."

15. See Armen A. Alchian, "Uncertainty, Evolution and Economic Theory," *Journal of Political Economy,* 58(3), June 1950, pp. 211–221.

16. M. Allais, "Le Comportement de l'Homme Rational Devant le Risque: Critiques de Postulates et Axioms de l'Ecole Americaine," *Econometrica,* October 1953, 21(4), pp. 503–546.

17. D. Kahneman and A. Tversky, "Prospect Theory: An Analysis of Decision Under Risk," *Econometrica,* 47, 1979, pp. 263–291.

18. David Grether and Charles Plott, "Economic Theory of Choice and the Preference Reversal Phenomenon," *American Economic Review,* 69(4), September 1979, pp. 623–638.

19. Richard Thaler, "Toward a Positive Theory of Consumer Choice," *Journal of Economic Behavior and Organization,* 1, 1981, pp. 39–60.

20. *Ibid.*

3

Why Are Free Markets So Good?

As we saw in chapter 1, one of the critical characteristics of the free market argument is its hypothesis that the market, if left alone, will generate socially desirable results. This hypothesis is supported by modern economic theorists, who have proven what have been called the Fundamental Theorems of Welfare Economics or the invisible hand theorems, which, in a restricted sense, prove Adam Smith's assertions to be correct. But exactly what are the advantages of organizing society along free market lines? What is the advantage of leaving individuals alone to barter and trade? One answer would be that this type of economic organization is the only one consistent with individual freedom. Milton Friedman echoes this view in *Capitalism and Freedom*, where he points out that there has never been a politically free society that did not have a capitalist economic system. Hence, for ideological reasons we should have a vested interest in maintaining our free enterprise system.[1] But there is a more fundamental economic reason why society should want its economy organized along the lines of the free market. This reason stems from the work of F. A. Hayek, who discusses the market as the most efficient mechanism capable of processing the huge amount of disparate information necessary to coordinate the plans of individual economic agents.[2] This defense of the market grew out of the debates in the 1930's between Hayek and Ludwig von Mises on the one hand and Oskar Lange and Abba Lerner on the other concerning the feasibility of market socialism. To illustrate these informational characteristics, consider the following anecdotes.

ANECDOTE 1

A man organized an elimination tennis tournament in which twenty players were to compete. Some were naturally better than others, and everyone in the tournament knew roughly how good the others were. In the first round all contestants played three opponents and those that won two out of three matches passed on to the remainder of the tournament. The organizer had to decide how to arrange the matches without arousing the anger of the players. Obviously, players wanted to play the weakest opponents to qualify for the remainder of the tournament, and yet someone had to play the better players. The organizer also wanted to arrange matches that would be as close as possible without having the best players eliminated early, since he expected many paying spectators. He had to choose a method of arranging matches that was fair and efficient in terms of maximizing spectator interest. In addition to solving these equity and efficiency problems, he also had to solve a rather involved mathematical combinatorial problem in which all twenty entrants play exactly three matches each and no player plays the same person more than once. When the organizer asked an economist for advice, he was told: "Do nothing. Just announce that entrants must find their own three first-round matches, and when they agree on whom they want to play, they should simply sign up. This scheme would have solved all of his problems. Each player would try to find the easiest three matches, and no player would agree to a match if there was a lesser player who would agree to play him. Since the matches were arranged voluntarily, players could not argue that they were assigned matches that were too hard—they had no one to blame but themselves.

Since players could refuse to play opponents who were obviously better than they, no mismatches would result, and the closeness and the spectator interest of each match would be maximized.

ANECDOTE 2

A professor of economics thought it might be efficient to arrange the seating of his class to maximize the amount of information transmitted. The seats in the front and middle of the room had the best view and acoustics, seats on the side next best, and seats in the back the worst. He first thought that he would ask his students how much they cared about learning the material and assign them to seats accordingly. But no students would admit that they did not care about the material for fear of insulting him and jeopardizing their grade. He then decided to give each student $100, had them stand in the back of the room, and auctioned off the seats to the highest bidder. He suspected he would find that students who cared about listening and seeing would bid high amounts for the seats up front, while students who did not care would bid only for the back seats, which would be sold at lesser prices. The students would then take the money left unspent on seats and spend it on other goods. As a result of this auction the market prices for seats determined by the bidding should allocate the students in exactly the way the professor would have done if he were given the correct information. By bidding for seats and sacrificing money that could be spent elsewhere, those students who cared about learning would be allocated to the front and those who did not (or who had an overriding need for the money) would be allocated to the back. The market would reveal all of the information that was needed to allocate students properly.

These anecdotes illustrate the advantages of the market organization of society. The competitive market is an extremely efficient information-processing device that allows individually scattered bits of local information known only to specialists to be exchanged at minimal cost in order to coordinate social activity efficiently. In our tennis example, the matching problem could have been solved effortlessly by the organizer had he simply trusted the selfish, utility-maximizing aims of the entrants and allowed them to process and weigh all of the information available to them. This solution is clearly more desirable than having him decide unilaterally about all matches, which would involve his evaluating the quality of each entrant in the contest and then finding matches for them. This information is most cheaply available to the players themselves. Each player is a specialist on his own ability. This information can be found out by a central planner only by lengthy and costly interviewing, all of which is subject to strategic manipulation and lying. Allowing the participants to make their own matches places the decision-making power in the hands of those who have the best information at their disposal. Hence, a better decision is guaranteed to result. Such an informational justification for the market is most clearly seen in the writings of F. A. Hayek.[3]

To see a more economically relevant argument for free markets, consider an economy with workers of varying abilities, caused either by heredity or the societal environment, and with entrepreneurs who are willing to enter the industries they expect to be most profitable. The workers and entrepreneurs supply their labor and capital in markets and earn wages and profits for their type of work that are set by the free market as they compete for employment and as firms compete for their services and investments.

The relevant economic questions are:

1. Which goods should be produced?
2. In what quantities should they be produced?
3. How should the worker's labor time be allocated to produce these various goods?
4. How should these goods be allocated to the workers and entrepreneurs?

If we use the example of the tennis tournament as an analogy, it should be clear that there are two ways to answer these questions. One is to allow a planner to make decisions by fiat, to provide a plan for how many shoes, candles, books, etc., the economy should produce in a given year, how workers should be allocated to produce this list given the existing technology, and how these goods, after being produced, should be allocated. Needless to say, this task would be difficult. The other way to proceed would be to do nothing. Simply allow the entrepreneurs to guess what people want, produce these goods, put them on the market, and adjust prices to fit actual demand. If the entrepreneurs choose to produce a product that no one wants, or if they produce too many products, their price will be low. As a result, the incomes of these producers will also be low, satisfaction with their production choice will be low, and some will switch to production of goods with higher expected profit. Until they do so, the economy will not be in equilibrium.

As a result of the economic signals produced by free-market prices, resources will be shifted by entrepreneurs away from those industries where profits are relatively low into those where profits are higher. However, since prices simply reflect the preferences of the consumers, we find the competitive process moving resources from low profit (low demand, high supply) industries to higher profit (high demand, low supply) industries, which is exactly what we would want if our objective is to satisfy the preferences of consumers.

There are many reasons why advocates of free markets prefer to have a free market rather than central planners allocate goods and services. One major reason concerns the objectives of planners. These people aim to produce and distribute goods according to their own preferences, their idea of what is right for society, or their perception of the preferences of the population. In any case, strong objections can be raised. In the first case, what moral argument can one raise to justify planners taking it upon themselves to allocate goods? After all, if one views society (as advocates of free markets do) as nothing more than an aggregation of individuals, then it should be the individuals' preferences that are reflected in the social allocation and not those of the planners. Consequently, if this logic is followed, the job of planners would be solely to implement the preferences of the individuals in society. But for several reasons even this role is superfluous. Any mechanism that tries to elicit individual preferences can be manipulated strategically by the individuals once they realize that their allocation will be affected by their response. Even if they report their preferences truthfully, Kenneth Arrow has shown that there is no consistent way to *aggregate* these preferences into a consistent set of social preferences.[4] Hence, the effort would be in vain. Even if all the above problems could be solved, collection and processing of this information would be prohibitively expensive.

The free market produces just the opposite result. Here, individual preferences can be expressed by bidding away resources from less preferred uses and allocating them to more preferred ones. In addition, individuals do not have an incentive to conceal their true preferences, because if they do, the resulting allocation is less preferable in their eyes. Finally, information on individual preferences is revealed and transmitted at minimal costs in the free market.

Hence, just as the tennis-tournament coordinator had a mandate to "match each player so as to maximize the quality of the matches," the market planner has a mandate to "allocate goods and services to satisfy individual preferences most completely." However, since preferences are expressed by individuals bidding for goods and services in the free market, maximizing individual preferences becomes synonymous with maximizing the value of goods and services produced (when those goods and services are valued at equilibrium prices that reflect society's preferences). Again, it appears that the answer must be the same—adopt a laissez-faire policy and all will turn out well.

The arguments for free markets are appealing. In the chapters that follow, however, we will investigate instances where these markets may not determine desirable outcomes, and we will discuss the reasons for these undesirable results. We hope that the reader will develop a more skeptical view of the unrestrained use of free markets as social mechanisms to cure our ills.

NOTES

1. See also William Simon, *A Time For Truth,* New York: McGraw-Hill, 1978, for a rather emotional endorsement of this point.
2. For a modern-day application of Hayek's ideas, see Thomas Sowell, *Knowledge and Decisions,* New York: Basic Books, 1981. For a good discussion of Hayek's ideas, see Gerald O'Driscoll, *Economics As a Coordinating Problem,* Kansas City: Sheed, Andres and MacNeel, 1977.
3. See F. A. Hayek, "Economics and Knowledge," *Economica,* 4, 1937, pp. 33–54.
4. Kenneth Arrow, *Individual Choice and Social Value,* 2nd ed., New York: Wiley, 1963.

4
Rationality and Market Failure

Just as in life "he who lives by the sword shall die by the sword," in economics "he who lives by rationality shall die by rationality." The very individual rationality that makes the market work so well often destroys the optimality of its results. In this chapter we will review cases illustrating this phenomenon. By focusing on rationality as the Achilles heel of the free market argument, we will shed new light on traditional laissez-faire arguments.

THE PRISONER'S DILEMMA

The most famous problem used by economists to demonstrate the self-defeating aspects of rational competition is the prisoner's dilemma game. Two robbers are caught as they finish robbing a store but after disposing of the goods. The police, believing they are guilty but lacking enough evidence to convict them, take them to the police station and interrogate them in separate rooms. Each robber is given a chance to confess to the crime. If neither confesses, the police cannot convict them of robbery but can convict them of the lesser crime of loitering at the scene of an accident. In this case both

ROBBER 2

		do not confess	confess
ROBBER 1	*do not confess*	6 months in jail, 6 months in jail	10 years in jail, 0 years in jail
	confess	0 years in jail, 10 years in jail	5 years in jail, 5 years in jail

Figure 4-1. The prisoner's dilemma

would go to jail for six months. However, if one confesses and the other does not, then the one that confesses will receive immunity for his cooperation in helping to convict the other. In this case, the squealer will get off with a fine, while the one who did not confess will go to jail for ten years. Finally, if they both confess, they will both be convicted, but because there was insubstantial evidence (remember they disposed of the goods), they will go to jail for only five years each on a lesser charge.

The decision problem for each player is portrayed in Figure 4-1. Notice that the worst outcome for any robber is not to confess and to have his partner confess, while the best is to confess while the partner does not. Also notice that the best strategy for the robbers if they act in unison is not to confess (six months in jail each) rather than to confess (five years in jail each).

Now, if both agents are rational and interested in maximizing their utility (i.e., minimizing the number of years they spend in jail), what decision will both robbers make? The answer is to confess. The reason is simple: If you were robber

1 and you knew that robber 2 would not confess, then your best response would be to confess. Then you would not go to jail at all, while if you did not confess you would go for six months. Similarly, if you knew that robber 2 were going to confess, your best response would again be to confess, because you would go to jail for five rather than ten years. Hence, regardless of what the other robber does, it is best for each to confess.

However, when both robbers confess they go to jail for five years, while if neither do they go for only six months. The point is that in this situation if each person acts rationally and pursues his own self-interest, the societal outcome is worse than if each individual does not. In short, the invisible hand of individual maximization seems to break down here—both robbers would be better off if they acted in a non-rational, socially minded manner.

This type of problem exists in many social settings. Consider a problem involving water pollution.[1] Say that two competing bottling companies operate factories on the shores of a lake whose waters they use to make their beverages. The lake can tolerate only 200 tons of waste without becoming so polluted that its water will be unfit for use. The companies can install either high- or low-cost waste-treatment plants. High-cost plants dump 90 tons of factory wastes into the lake, while low-cost plants dump 110 tons. The payoffs to the firms are as follows: If both use the high-cost filtering system, then the lake will be less polluted and each plant can use the lake's waters. In this case, the profits of the firms will be $1,000,000 each. If they both use the low-cost waste-treatment plant, the lake will be so polluted that both will have to treat the *water* as well before using it. This treatment represents an extra cost and profits will drop to $600,000 each. Finally, if one uses the low-cost and one the high-cost waste-treatment plant, water treatment will not be necessary. However, the firm using the low-cost waste-treatment plant will produce its beverage at a lower unit cost and will be able to under-price its high-cost rival. The low-cost firm will make $1,200,000 in profits, while the high-cost firm will make only $500,000. The situation is analogous to the prisoner's-dilemma game and is

FIRM 2

	use high-cost plant	use low-cost plant
FIRM 1 use high-cost plant	$1,000,000 $1,000,000	$500,000 $1,200,000
use low-cost plant	$1,200,000 $500,000	$600,000 $600,000

Figure 4–2. Potential outcomes of the water-pollution problem

represented in Figure 4–2 (the top number in each box is the payoff to firm 1 and the bottom number the payoff to firm 2).

If both firms are rational, they will both build low-cost treatment plants, the lake will be polluted, and their profits will be $600,000 each, instead of the $1,000,000 they could make if they both used the high-cost treatment plant. Thus, we have a classic case of individual rationality leading to group irrationality. By trying to maximize their individual profits, the companies end up minimizing their joint profits and seriously polluting a lake.

What could solve this problem and restore the optimality of individual utility maximization? First, a legal system could help. If the firms could both agree to build high-cost plants, and if this agreement could be enforced as a binding contract in a court of law, then the problem would disappear. However, although producing such a contract may be practical with two firms, doing so with 100 firms would be much more difficult.

At this point the belief of free-market advocates in property rights asserts itself. Using the arguments of Ronald Coase, these people would argue that the hypothetical situation does not represent a market failure but an institutional failure, since if property rights to use the lake's water were fully allocated, the lake would be clean.[2] If firm 1 owned the water rights to the lake, then firm 2 would have to pay firm 1 to use the lake. In their negotiations, however, firm 1 would most likely insist that firm 2 use the high-cost treatment plant. Firm 1 would then use the low-cost plant, the lake would be cleaner, and the jointly disastrous economic result would be avoided. If firm 2 had the property rights, the opposite would happen. Consequently, as long as the rights are assigned (no matter to whom), the lake remains clean. All that varies is the distribution of profits.

This solution, however, has some serious problems. One is that it may be impossible or extremely undesirable to assign property rights to individuals. Any effort to auction off, say, the air we breath or Lake Michigan to the highest bidder would probably meet with great resistance because of its potential antisocial effects. Even if property rights are assigned, such a scheme is again likely to work well only in the case of a small number of agents who can negotiate at minimal cost with the owner of the property rights for the use of the resource he owns. If negotiations are costly, the rights may not be used properly and their whole *raison d'être* would be nullified. Ultimately, situations of the type described here cannot be avoided very easily. While the market must rely on humanity's selfish rationality to function, it must also bear the consequences of that rationality on a daily basis.

RATIONALITY, MARKETS WITH ASYMMETRIC INFORMATION, AND ETHICAL HAZARD

One of the defining characteristics of perfectly competitive markets is the assumption of complete information. Under this assumption, if all firms and consumers are fully and symmetrically informed (i.e., consumers know exactly what firms do about all prices and opportunities in the market) and fully

rational, then no unexploited profit opportunities can exist
and the market outcome will be optimal in the long run.

Recently, however, through the works of Akerlof, Rothschild and Stiglitz, Wilson, and Pitchik and Schotter, to men-
tion just a few, economists have learned that when information
is asymmetric, markets can break down and such breakdowns
can create a need for market intervention.[3]

To understand how this might happen, consider a town
with car owners and service stations. On a given day all cars
break down and have either a major or a minor problem. If a
car has a major problem, any service station will charge the
owner $450 to fix it. If it has a minor problem, any station
will charge $350. It costs the stations $250 to fix a major
problem and $150 to fix a minor problem.

Since car owners are ignorant of the cause of their car's
problem, they have to depend on service station owners for an
opinion before deciding which repair to buy (this obviously is
analogous to the problem of searching for a medical diagnosis). After testing the car on their diagnostic machine, the
service station owners identify the problem. But since they
know that the consumers do not know what is wrong (i.e.,
there is asymmetrical information), the service station owners have a great incentive to lie and diagnose the problem as
major when it is not. Thus profit-maximizing rational firms
face a situation of "ethical hazard"—they have an incentive to
lie.

Finally, assume that 50 percent of the firms are incompetent and have machines that diagnose correctly only 80 percent of the time. In such a market, a consumer who gets an
opinion does not know whether it is from a firm that is competent and honest, incompetent and honest, competent and dishonest, or incompetent and dishonest.

Pitchik and Schotter have proven that in markets with
these characteristics the temptation to lie may be too great
for rational firms to resist.[4] In fact, for every market of this
general description, an equilibrium always exists in which all
firms (competent and incompetent) are totally dishonest. If
such an equilibrium does emerge, a clear case for government
intervention can be made, since we have another example of a

situation in which rationality ruins the market. However, such an equilibrium is not inevitable, since others are possible in which there may be quite high levels of honesty among both the competent and incompetent firms. The exact equilibrium established depends on the parameters of the market (i.e., the price of a major and minor repair, the cost of these repairs, the fraction of competent firms in the market, etc.). Using the numbers in the example above, an equilibrium exists in which 95 percent of the incompetents and 60 percent of the competents are honest. Consequently, whether government intervention is needed in these markets depends on the type of professional ethic that emerges among the experts in the market. If the ethic involves high levels of honesty, all is well. If not, the only alternative is regulation. Notice, however, that even in the best-case scenario the market needs more than individual rationality to obtain optimal or satisfactory results. It needs a shared social ethic that all experts adhere to in order to function properly. Hence, while individual rationality may be necessary for the proper functioning of markets, it certainly is not sufficient for that purpose.

RATIONALITY, MARKETS WITH ASYMMETRIC INFORMATION, AND ADVERSE SELECTION: THE "LEMON" PROBLEM

In "The Market for Lemons: Quality, Uncertainty and Market Mechanism," his seminal article on markets with asymmetric information, George Akerlof identifies situations in which such markets can fail. They do so in the sense that no transaction takes place despite the fact that there are traders in the market for whom such trades would be mutually beneficial. When we look at his model we again see that it is individual rationality, this time coupled with asymmetric information, that spoils the free market outcome. To understand the argument, assume a town with used-car owners and with potential buyers of these cars. The cars vary in quality from very good to very bad, but only the owners know their car's quality. Since the potential buyers know nothing, they must assume that the car they look at has the average quality of cars on the market. Hence, they are willing to pay at most the price of an average car. However, at that price only sellers with cars of quality less than the average would be willing to sell. The car buyers thus know that any car they buy must be of below average quality, so they would be paying too much for it and would not buy. Hence, at any price either buyers or sellers would be unwilling to transact business and the market would be inactive. The bad cars drive out the good, despite the fact that if information were perfect there would be many trades.

The upshot of this argument is that such markets may be prime candidates for government intervention and control. Car dealers must be licensed and car quality verified if the market is going to function properly.

RATIONALITY AND EXTERNALITIES

When Adam Smith theorized about the free market, he envisioned an economy composed of a multitude of isolated individuals, each of whom pursued his or her own self-interest and none of whom interfered with anyone else's pursuit of self-interest except, of course, through competition in the market. It was as if all people were islands unto themselves, tied to other islands by an impersonal market. However, the world is not like that. My act of production or consumption is very likely to affect you in many ways, some of which you may like and some you may not. Assume that I own a factory situated near a hotel that you own. My factory has smokestacks hidden by tall trees. The only evidence of my hotel's existence to your guests is the soot from my smokestacks, which falls on them as they try to sunbathe. Clearly, I am not an island unto myself. My act of production has several detrimental effects on you and your guests. These effects can be called externalities, since they are costs borne by people external to the person who generates them—you, the hotel owner, and not me, the factory owner.

Take another example. Say that you and I live in adjacent suburban houses. One day, you decide to hire an architect to

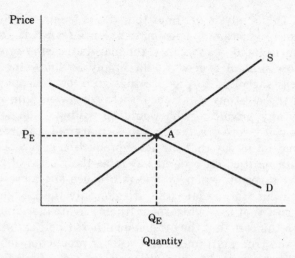

Figure 4–3. Supply and demand curves under perfect competition

landscape your lot. The result turns out to be smashing—so smashing, in fact, that the entire street looks better and the prices of all of our houses rise, including mine. Obviously, you were not the only one who benefited from your expenditures— you generated positive externalities. Again, less separates us than an impersonal market.

Now what problem do these externalities create for the proper functioning of competitive markets with self-interested rational agents? Remember that basic economics teaches us that the equilibrium price in a perfectly competitive market is determined at the point of intersection of the supply and the demand curve (see Figure 4–3). This price and the associated quantity are supposed to be optimal for society because the supply curve of a competitive industry represents the marginal cost of producing various units, while the demand curve represents the marginal benefit of consuming these units. Hence, only at point A, where the two curves intersect, is the marginal cost of producing one more unit equal to the marginal benefit and societal utility maximized.

But this analysis assumes that there are no externalities in either production or consumption. For instance, if everyone lived on isolated islands, then the marginal cost of producing one more unit of a good would simply be the value of the resources sacrificed to produce that good (or the opportunity cost of those resources). Hence, these costs would have to be met by any producer, who would be willing to do so if the market price were greater than these marginal resource costs. However, let us say that the act of production generates negative externalities on others that raise their costs of production. As a result, when producers produce one more unit of their output, the social costs are not only the marginal resource cost that they must incur (their private marginal cost), but also the cost that they inflict on others (their externality). Hence the true marginal social costs of production for a firm generating externalities is different from the marginal private costs it has to meet.

This fact is significant because, coupled with individual rationality, it is capable of ruining the optimality of market outcomes. If the market functioned optimally, it would produce that amount of a good for which the societal marginal benefit equaled the societal marginal cost. When no externalities exist, this is exactly what markets do, because in those cases there is no difference between marginal private and marginal social costs. But when negative externalities exist, we can see that markets will provide more goods than is socially optimal (see Figure 4–4). Here we see the market output (*P market* – *Q market*) occurring at the intersection of the supply curve (marginal private cost curve) and demand curve. The optimum output, however, occurs at (*P optimal* – *Q optimal*)—the intersection of the marginal social cost and demand curves. This conclusion follows from the assumption of individual rationality, because if firms maximize their private profits, they will all equate their marginal private costs to the price they receive for the good. This will then generate the supply curve labelled in Figure 4–4. However, society is best off when firms equate the price they get for their good to the marginal social costs of production, because this best reflects what society must sacrifice to supply one more unit of

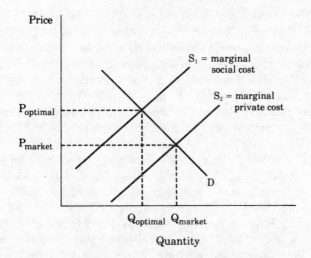

Figure 4–4. Overproduction caused by negative externalities

the good. Consequently, individual rationality has spoiled the market again. Since each producer cares only about his own private marginal costs of production, he has no incentive to consider the costs he is inflicting on others every time he produces another unit. What is best for each individual is not what is best for the society, and again some extra-market institution (property rights, tax law, pollution quotas, effluent charges, etc.) is needed to rectify the mess made by individual utility maximization.

PUBLIC GOODS: RATIONALITY AND FREE RIDING

There are basically two types of economic goods—public goods and private goods. A private good has the property that one person's consumption of it totally precludes anyone else from consuming it. For instance, an apple is a purely private good, since my eating it excludes anyone else from doing so. Adam

Smith was thinking about markets for private goods when he spoke of the benefits of the invisible hand. The reason that these markets should work so well is quite simple. Say someone wants to sell an apple and there are two potential buyers. The seller would sell to any buyer who offers more than fifty cents. Buyer 1 is willing to pay up to $1.00, while buyer 2 is willing to pay up to $1.50. We will call an allocation optimal if it allocates the good to the buyer who is willing to pay the most for it. The seller of the apple holds an auction and the two buyers bid for it openly. Clearly the apple will be sold to buyer 2, because if he bids less than buyer 1 he will not win the apple and, because it is a private good, he will lose the utility he could receive from eating it. Hence, he has an incentive to keep on bidding (up to $1.50, if necessary) until he wins the apple. In other words, because the apple is a private good and he will be excluded from its use if he loses the bidding, he has an incentive to reveal to the market (through his bids) how much he is willing to pay for the apple. Hence, the allocation must be optimal.

Now the analysis of markets for public goods is quite different. First of all, a person's consumption of a pure public good does not diminish any other person's consumption. In addition, once the good is produced, no one can be excluded from its use. The typical example of a public good is national defense. Clearly, if I live in a city that is defended by an antiballistic missile system, then the fact that that system is protecting me (or that I am "consuming" it) does not diminish the degree to which it protects anyone else (their consumption). Once constructed, the system protects all people who live in the city.

When we study markets for public goods, we see that once again individual rationality ruins the optimality feature of the market. Say you live on a dark city street in a high-crime neighborhood and that your block association (a voluntary group of neighbors) decides to get together and light the street. In buying the lighting, the association finds that the more money it spends, the brighter the street light. The question then is: What is the optimal intensity of lighting to buy? If the association knows how much money each member would be willing to spend on various lighting levels, it would simply pick that level at which the sum of the willingness to pay for the last intensity unit bought equalled the marginal cost of providing that unit. This is the optimal level. But will a market provide this answer? Consider how the association might go about getting the information it needs to make its decision. If it tries the simplest approach, merely asking its members how much they would be willing to spend for lighting, the simultaneous existence of individual rationality and the non-excludable quality of the good being bought would make it unlikely that the optimal amount would be provided. As a rational and self-interested member of the association, you would realize that once the street association installed the street lights you would benefit from them whether you contributed or not—the lighting is a public good. In fact, if you do not contribute at all, you get two benefits: you are protected by lights provided for you free of charge, and you can spend on private goods the money you would have contributed. Consequently, when asked to contribute, you might be tempted to reply, "I think the whole idea of street lighting is wrong. I won't give anything." If all people are rational and act this way, the good will not be provided, despite the fact that all people want it. The problem then is that markets for public goods lack the incentives for people to reveal their true willingness to pay for the goods that exist in markets for private goods, because rational people know that they can not be excluded from using a public good provided by the other agents in society and are tempted to get a free ride.

There are two ways out of this bind. In many situations where free rides are possible, a social convention develops in which people report their true willingness to pay despite their private incentives to cheat. For example, many European public transportation systems have virtually unpoliced rider payment systems, yet people contribute willingly. Sometimes payment for public goods can be supported by social sanctions or explicit punishments. Here, as in the case of the market with asymmetric information, a social institution or convention to supplement the market is required to achieve socially optimal results.

If such a beneficial institution is not developed, then some type of collective or state action is required. Recently, economists have turned their attention to designing mechanisms for allocating public goods that lead people to report their true willingness to pay. The ironic aspect of these mechanisms is that they rely on each agent's individual rationality to insure that they elicit the truth from everyone, so that exactly the element that ruins the market allows collective intervention to patch it up. Let us see how this can be true.

Assume that the president of our street association asks members to pick from three different lighting plans—plan A (one street light), plan B (two street lights), and plan C (three street lights). Each plan costs the same amount of money. There are only four people on the street, persons 1, 2, 3 and 4, and their true willingness to pay is displayed in Figure 4–5. This table tells us, for instance, that person 3 most prefers having only two lights on the streets and would be willing to

	PLANS			
	A	B	C	Tax
1	60	50	40	0
2	30	70	50	5
3	20	80	25	4
4	40	20	90	0
Total willingness to pay	150	220	205	

PERSONS

Figure 4–5. Willingness to pay of association members

contribute up to $80 for plan B, but would be willing to contribute only $20 for plan A (he thinks it will do little good) and $25 for plan C (he fears the lights will prevent him from sleeping).

The problem now is to devise a scheme that will force the members of the street association to report the truth and consequently allow the president to choose the appropriate or optimal plan. From our free market utilitarian assumption of chapter 2, "optimal" here will be taken to mean the plan that maximizes the difference between the total amount people are willing to pay for a plan and its cost. However, since we assume all costs to be the same, the optimal plan is simply the one that maximizes the neighbor's willingness to pay. Hence, the optimal plan is plan B, whose total willingness to pay is $220 as opposed to $150 for plan A and $205 for plan C.

Such a scheme, which was first investigated by William Vickrey, Theodore Groves, Edward Clarke, and Nicholas Tideman and G. Tullock, was labeled the demand-revealing scheme or mechanism.[5] Following Tideman and Tullock's exposition, let us see how such a scheme would work. First, let each member of the street association write down the maximum amount of money he would be willing to pay to have each of the three plans adopted. Accepting this information as true, the president would then simply choose that project whose net benefits—reported willingness to pay minus cost— was greatest. Hence, the first part of the mechanism is trivial. Next, we must specify how much each neighbor is going to pay (i.e., his tax). Consider the project that is chosen when any neighbor's message is included in the president's calculations and when it is not. In other words, look at the project that would be chosen both in the case where this neighbor is a member of the street association and where he is not. If the same plan is chosen in both cases, then this neighbor's message to the president does not change the association's decision and he is to be taxed nothing. If his message does change the association's choice, then he is to be taxed the difference between the total willingness to pay for the best choice of the three-person association defined without him and the willingness to pay for the project that is chosen with him. For instance, in Figure 4–5, if all neighbors reported truthfully to the president, the taxes would be nothing for person 1, $5 for 2, $4 for 3, and nothing for 4. This is derived as follows: If all people report truthfully, plan B will be chosen, since the sum of the reported willingness to pay for B is greatest. Notice that if we eliminate person 1 from the association, then the total willingness to pay for plan A is $90, for B is $170, and for C is $165. Plan B is chosen either with person 1's message or without it. Hence, 1's tax is $0. Now look at person 2. When her message is included, the association's choice is B. However, when her message is eliminated the association's choice is C, which receives a total of $155 as opposed to $150 for B and $120 for A. Hence, 2's message changes the social choice from C to B, and she is taxed the difference between the $155 bid for C and the $150 bid for B in the association without her. Similar calculations are made for persons 3 and 4.

It has been shown that if this scheme were to be used and if all agents were rational and interested only in their own selfish payoffs, the best thing they could do would be to report their true willingness to pay to the president of the association. Consequently, he would receive exactly the right information necessary to choose the optimal lighting plan. The scheme constructively harnesses individual rationality toward the social good, which it would not do without the scheme.

But why does the scheme work? Why would our selfish, utility-maximizing neighbors be forced to tell the truth by this scheme? To understand, let us look at person 3's calculations. He likes plan B the most, then plan C, then plan A.

Let us say that the three other people submit messages such that the association president would choose plan B if there were only three members. In this case, it would clearly be best for person 3 to submit a truthful message, since if he does, project B (his first choice) will be chosen and he will not have to pay any tax for it. If he were to lie and say he would be willing to pay more for A or C, he would then run the risk of changing the association's choice from B to something else and he would be taxed as well.

Now say that the other three members send messages

such that project C would be chosen without person 3. Then if person 3 submits information that keeps the social choice at C, he will not be taxed, C will be chosen, and his net benefit will be $25 ($25 minus a tax of zero). If C is the alternative of society, then person 3's tax will be independent of his message, no matter what he says. Say that he is contemplating sending a message that changes the alternative from C to B. If this is so his tax will be either more than $55 or less than $55. If it is more than $55, then he would be better off to tell the truth and let C remain as the social alternative, since his payoff from changing the social alternative from C to B will be less than $25–the payoff achieved when C is chosen and 3 is not taxed. Likewise, if 3's tax is less than $55, he is better off reporting his true preference, because then B will be chosen and his tax will be less than $55, which means that his payoff will be more than $25. This line of thinking indicates that when such a demand-revealing mechanism is used, honesty becomes the best policy among a set of rational economic agents.

NOTES

1. R. Hardin, "Collective Action as an Agreeable n-Prisoner's Dilemma," *Behavioral Science*, 16, September 1971, pp. 472–481.
2. Ronald Coase, "The Problem of Special Cost," *Journal of Law and Economics*, 3, 1960, pp. 1–44.
3. See Michael Rothschild and Joseph Stiglitz, "Equilibrium in Competitive Insurance Markets: An Essay on the Economics of Imperfect Competition," *Quarterly Journal of Economics*, 90(4), 1976, pp. 629–649; Charles Wilson, "Model of Insurance Markets with Incomplete Information," *Journal of Economic Theory*, 16(2), October 1977, pp. 167–207; and Carolyn Pitchik and Andrew Schotter, "Internal and External Regulation of Markets with Asymmetric Information," unpublished paper at NYU, second revision, April 1983.
4. Pitchik and Schotter, "Internal and External Regulation."
5. See William Vickrey, "Counter Speculation, Auctions and Competitive Sealed Tenders," *Journal of Finance*, 16, pp. 8–37; Theodore Groves, "Incentives in Teams," *Econometrica*, 41, July

1973, pp. 617–631; Edward Clarke, "Multipart Pricing of Public Goods," *Public Choice,* 11, pp. 17–33; and Nicholas Tideman and Gordon Tullock, "A New and Superior Process for Making Social Choices," *Journal of Political Economy,* 84, 1976, pp. 1145–1159.

5

Free Market Policy Prescriptions

Free market efficiency arguments are often used as justifications for policies that strike many people as unfair, unequitable, or cold-hearted. Debates of these arguments tend to go nowhere because the participants argue at cross purposes. In this chapter I will look at some common free market arguments concerning such issues as the minimum wage, educational vouchers, crime, and anti-discrimination laws and present efficiency-type arguments that could be used to counter the free market position on these issues. In short, I will present some "immanent" criticisms of free market policies by accepting the assumptions upon which these policies are based and following their logic one step beyond that contemplated by typical policy makers. We will discover that in many cases what at first appeared to be an efficient policy may turn out to be quite counterproductive.

CORNER SOLUTIONS, RATIONALITY, CRIME, AND THE MINIMUM WAGE

From our previous discussion, it would appear that markets are optimal allocating mechanisms except for a few instances in which externalities, asymmetric information, or public goods are present. In this section, however, I will look at a circumstance in which the market fails even in the absence of these other factors. Ironically, we will see that the market can do its job too well and the optimal free market solution turn out to be what economists call a "corner solution." Such solutions, while mathematically satisfactory, may be socially undesirable. To explain corner solutions, let us look at an old military example that was one of the first applications of a mathematical tool called linear programming. Assume that you have an army you must feed. A nutritionist has estimated that every soldier needs 70 grams of protein and 10 milligrams of iron a day. Three foods are available: peanut butter, Spam, and Jello, each of which has these two nutrients in fixed amounts. For every ounce of Spam one eats, one gets 20 gm. of protein and 3 mg. of iron. Each ounce of peanut butter has 40 gm. of protein and 4 mg. of iron, and each ounce of Jello 60 gm. of protein and 1 mg. of iron. The army wants to supply these daily minimum requirements at the least cost. Spam costs 50 cents an ounce, peanut butter 20 cents an ounce, and Jello 30 cents an ounce. The army's problem is to buy that bundle of Spam, peanut butter, and Jello that will supply the army's soldiers with the minimum daily requirements at the least cost. It is a simple cost-minimization problem subject to the constraints that certain minimum daily requirements are satisfied, much as the economic planning problem of chapter 3 was a GNP-maximization problem subject to resource, labor, and technological constraints and our tennis problem of chapter 3 was spectator-interest-maximization problem. But if we start to investigate what characteristics the solution to such a problem would have, one conclusion would be immediately clear. The army would never buy any Spam because, ounce for ounce, peanut butter gives more protein and iron and is cheaper. Any solution to a maximization or minimization problem such as this one in which one or more of the variables in the problem (i.e., Spam here) is given a zero value is called a "corner solution" because it lies at the corner of the set of all possible solution values.

Now, let us look at the relationship of this concept to the economic planning problem studied in chapter 3. In the economy described there, the social planner was asked to maximize the value of goods and services produced subject to the resource, labor, and technological constraints he faced. The laissez-faire solution to this situation also solves the same maximization problem but more efficiently. In other words, the free market would produce as many shoes, books, and candles as under the planner. The free market would produce these things using the same techniques and it would allocate them to the same people as the planner. The only difference would be that the market would determine these allocations by defining prices and wages that simultaneously furnish each agent in the economy with an income. But it may turn out that the optimal solution to this problem may be a corner solution in which the incomes of some workers may be practically zero or at least below the poverty level. This will be true because, like Spam in our diet problem, it is just not efficient for any firm to hire a certain type of labor at a positive or above-poverty wage because of their abilities (in the case of Spam, because of their nutritional value and price). Hence, the incomes of some workers will either be zero or a very low wage. This is not a fanciful theoretical possibility. For instance, in countries such as India and Bangladesh the number of unskilled workers is so high that efficiency would dictate paying unskilled workers a zero or near-zero wage. In economic jargon, their "shadow wage" is zero. Hence, those workers would face starvation for the sake of economic efficiency. A corner solution would be optimal. It costs money to keep these workers alive. But since there are so many of them, more than could be employed given the other resources and technological constraints, most of them are superfluous and add nothing to the economy. This fact is reflected by supply and demand in the market as a zero wage for these workers.

The existence of corner solutions creates several problems for economies whose agents are assumed to be rational. First is the obvious problem that such economies may face high unemployment rates and possibly starvation on a large scale. Second, and less obviously, one must ask what the rational response of "corner dwellers" to their plight would be. It is implicitly assumed in the economics literature that they are forced either to accept welfare or other types of state assistance or retrain themselves in order to escape their structural unemployment. However, as we shall see, there may be other, more antisocial, responses than these to the corner solution that may force us to modify some of our most dearly held free market ideas. To investigate this problem more fully, let us first discuss the relationship of crime and corner solutions and then look at that old chestnut, the minimum-wage debate.

THE LABOR MARKET, CRIME, POVERTY, AND CORNER SOLUTIONS

The labor market serves one and only one purpose in the economy—to match workers with jobs in the most efficient manner. If there are excess bricklayers in New Hampshire and a shortage of bricklayers in Colorado, the market should allocate bricklayers to Colorado by making the Colorado bricklayer wages high enough to induce New Hampshire bricklayers to move. As in our tennis tournament example, the best way to achieve this is to do nothing and allow the market to do its job, since then and only then can we be sure that people are allocated in a manner that maximizes the value of what is produced. At any particular time, given the technology that the economy employs, there is a demand for the services or goods produced by workers of particular types—doctors, accountants, auto workers, etc. These derived demands for workers are juxtaposed against the corresponding supplies to determine the wages that are set for their services in the market. As demand for certain types of products increases, the demand for the workers who produce these products also increases and hence their wages increase. As a result, the workers who have the skills to enter these industries do so and benefit from this increasing demand. They respond to the price and wage signals that the market sends out by allocating their time to working in various industries.

Consequently, in the labor market workers behave very much like business firms by entering those industries that seem most profitable in terms of wages and leaving those industries that do not. Of course, this is not always easily done. A truck driver does not become a doctor overnight because of the incentive of a doctor's income, and an accountant doesn't become a professional baseball player on the basis of Reggie Jackson's salary. There are barriers to entry into many fields and few people have the ability to transform themselves instantaneously.

Given these transformational constraints rational workers must decide how to allocate their time to a variety of activities that may include honest work, schooling or vocational training, reading, movie watching, and crime. For a rational economic agent, the problem is a straightforward maximization problem, quite familiar to economists, whose solution would dictate that the amount of time allocated to these various activities naturally depends on the relative prices and wages an agent faces. One in a high-wage industry may decide to spend a great deal of time working and less time watching movies, since the opportunity cost he faces when he watches movies is great. Likewise, the cost of leisure to a person facing an extremely low wage may be so low that he may decide to consume a great deal of it and work very little (since the wage does not compensate him for the unpleasantness of the work).

Depending upon the existing demands and supplies at any time, wages are set for every worker and define their incomes. But the optimal set of wages may involve a corner solution, in which the market is efficient if certain workers are given poverty or below poverty wages. This problem is obviously aggravated by the illegal immigration of workers, which increases the supply of low-skilled labor. In addition, the market will not provide capital to workers to allow them to train themselves. What will a rational person do in such circumstances? The answer can be found in the time-allocation problem described above. A worker responds in allocating his time to the wages and prices that he faces. After weighing all of the probabilities, profitabilities, and costs, a worker who is facing a below-poverty wage may rationally decide to allocate some of his time to illegal activities, such as running numbers, prostitution, gambling, burglary, purse snatching, pocket picking, and mugging. It is not true that as soon as a person's wage drops below a certain point he runs out into the street and commits crimes—most people just work harder. Rather, the amount of crime we experience is *to some extent* a function of the *relative* wages that people face (i.e., the relative criminal and non-criminal wage rates). For some people who have less aversion to committing crimes than others, a rational response is to allocate some of their time to criminal activity.

Hence, one way to view criminals is as utility-maximizing entrepreneurs who face various wages and prices and who allocate their time optimally between criminal and non-criminal activity. This view of criminal activity is precisely that taken by the Chicago School of economists, such as Gary Becker and Isaac Erlich, and is most consistent with the assumptions of the free market argument. The interesting thing about crime is that it is one of those industries that has the lowest educational barriers to entry and hence is very attractive to the structurally unemployed. When the demand for engineers in North Dakota or for accountants in Phoenix increases, unemployed youths do not move there because they are barred educationally from taking those types of jobs. One tempting field from which they are not barred, given their abilities, is the crime industry.

Hence, in a perfectly competitive economy, there may be at the prevailing "optimal" wage distribution a certain segment of the population that faces near-poverty wages. No existing economic theory can refute this claim, for all economists know that at the equilibrium of a perfectly competitive economy, some people may earn only a subsistence wage. If the legal wages faced by this segment of the population are at poverty or near-poverty levels (i.e., if a corner solution exists), the rational response of these people may be to allocate a portion of their time away from legal market-oriented activities and toward illegal activities such as crime, or non-market activities. Hence, one result of a corner solution is crime or other types of undesirable social behavior, which is clearly not contemplated by advocates of free markets subscribing to the axioms stated in chapter 1.

The existence of such corner solutions and the crime associated with them is obviously an important factor to consider when discussing the proper role of government intervention in free labor markets. Consequently, we must ask: What statistical calculation could we make, using the available data, that would convince us that the free market solution in the United States today involves a corner solution that relegates a certain portion of the population to the position of corner dwellers? Obviously, if we could substantiate the fact that a segment of the population is paid an extremely low wage (say, below $1.00 per hour) then this would be all the proof we would need.

But such a severe test is not realistic or even necessary for several reasons. First, there are institutional barriers such as minimum-wage laws, customs, norms, and employers' sense of fairness that prevent employers from offering zero or near-zero wages. Second, wages for certain groups in the United States are prevented from falling because people simply would refuse to offer their labor on the market, a situation usually described as the discouraged-worker phenomenon. Finally, it may not even benefit the profit-maximizing employers to pay zero wages, since workers living on wages below subsistence would most likely be too weak to perform their jobs adequately. Thus, the corner solution discussed above is a theoretical solution towards which the market for low-skilled labor gravitates, not necessarily a description of the real world.

In further investigating the labor market for low-skilled workers, we must answer the following question: If low-skilled workers did not get discouraged by low wages and withdraw their services from the market (i.e., if they offered their services no matter what wage they received), how low would the wage have to drop in order to employ all of them? To answer this question we first will have to examine the workings of the low-skilled labor market. In the analysis of

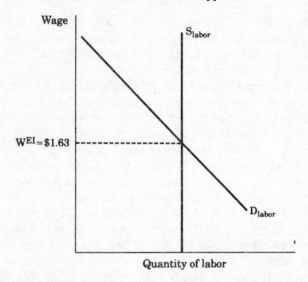

Figure 5-1. Wage

S$_{labor}$

W^{EI}=\$1.63

D$_{labor}$

Quantity of labor

Figure 5-1. Equilibrium wage for low-skilled workers

any market, the juxtaposition of supply and demand determines the equilibrium level of the wage. In Figure 5-1, demand is represented by a demand curve D$_{labor}$. This curve represents the fact that at each wage firms calculate how much labor they want to hire based upon profit-maximizing considerations. As the wage falls, it becomes profitable for them to hire more labor and, as a result, D$_{labor}$ is depicted as a curve that slopes downward and to the right. S$_{labor}$ depicts what the labor supply curve would look like if all low-skilled laborers offered their services to the market no matter what wage they received. Since there is no sensitivity to the wage in the labor-supply decision, that labor supply is depicted as a vertical curve. Under these assumptions, the intersection of D$_{labor}$ and S$_{labor}$ depicts what the equilibrium wage for low-skilled labor would be if workers were insensitive to the wage they received from work—about \$1.63 an hour, as I have calculated it. Though this is an exceedingly low wage rate, it represents a rather high estimate of the efficiency wage of this type of labor. It is the free market low-skill wage toward which the economy would strive if not interfered with. The only reason that we do not observe this wage, aside from the minimum-wage barrier, is that many workers would refuse to work at such low wages. Hence, in Figure 5–2, we depict what the labor supply curve would look like if workers were sensitive to the wage rate and offered more of their labor to the market as the wage rate increased and less as the wage rate fell. To depict this fact, the curve slopes upward and to the right. Figure 5–2 juxtaposes our wage-sensitive labor supply curve to the original demand curve to demonstrate that the wage sensitivity of these workers keeps the equilibrium wage above the market-efficiency wage depicted in Figure 5–1. Hence workers who are discouraged and drop out of the market allow the wage rate for low-skilled workers to rise above their efficiency levels.

No doubt free market theorists would take great exception to this interpretation, insisting that the only relevant equilibrium wage to look at is the one depicted in Figure 5–2—de-

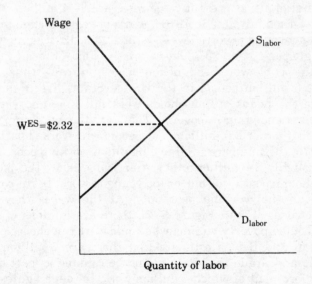

Figure 5–2. Equilibrium wage for low-skilled, wage-rate-sensitive workers

rived under the realistic assumption of wage sensitivity—since at that wage all workers *who want to work* can find a job. This is the definition of a "market-clearing wage." Their argument goes that if workers do not want to work at the going equilibrium wage, that is their problem. While they should not be forced to work, others who do work should not be forced to bail them out with income transfers. This argument, although consistent with the individualistic assumption of the free market argument, misses the point that what happens to these people is *everyone's* problem. Let us look at the decisions low-skilled people make when they are offered various wages. When low-skilled workers are willing to work for any wage as depicted in Figure 5–1, the equilibrium wage W^{EI} is obviously going to be lower than the wage we actually observe in the real world, where workers are wage-sensitive (as in Figure 5–2). Hence, the facts that I am about to describe would undoubtedly be worse if all institutional and psychological barriers were removed from the labor market and the actual wage were allowed to converge toward the theoretical wage W^{EI}.

First of all, at present wage rates nearly 4 million Americans worked full time in 1976 and did not earn enough to raise them above the poverty level—estimated in 1979 as $3,400 for a single person and $6,700 for a family of four. Since 1 million of these people were heads of households, one can estimate that about 6 million people in the United States live in families where the heads of households work full time and yet nevertheless ended up in poverty. These are the working poor. If we add another 2.6 million poor people who worked part time in 1976, the numbers swell to 8.6 million working poor. There are roughly 14 million other Americans below the poverty threshold too sick, too old, or too young to work. Let us concentrate on the working poor only. At the wages they earn (depicted as W^{ES} in Figure 5–2), there are millions of other able-bodied poverty victims who could work but choose not to. Levitan and Belous estimate that there are 7 million such people and argue that they should be counted as part of our labor force, out of which 4 million work. In rough figures, this leaves 3 million discouraged workers in 1976.

Let us then imagine that these 3 million workers decide

all at once to offer their labor on the market, and that all minimum-wage legislation is removed so that the wage could fall to its equilibrium level. Let us look at what would happen to the average wage of workers who earn less than $2.99 in 1976, when the minimum wage was $2.90. At that time there were 10.6 million workers who earned wages less than $2.99, with an average wage of approximately $2.32. To see what would happen if an additional 3 million workers entered the market and offered their labor at any market-clearing wage, we can use the work of Zucker, who estimates that the wage sensitivity of the demand elasticity for low-skilled labor is unity—for each 1 percent the wage falls, the demand for labor increases by 1 percent.[1] Hence, if an additional 3 million workers offered their labor services on the market, the wage would have to fall by 30 percent or to about $1.63 in order for all of these extra workers to be hired.[2] A wage of $1.63 an hour constitutes a weekly wage of approximately $65.20 for a 40-hour week job (if in fact such steady employment were possible for such low-wage jobs). For a person working 50 weeks a year this yields an annual salary of $3,260. Hence a family of four with two full-time low-wage workers working 40 hours a week 50 weeks a year would not be able to lift themselves out of poverty (especially when we consider that taxes are withheld from their wages as well). As a consequence, such low-wage rates do not exist on the labor market today because many workers refuse to work for them and as a result leave the labor market.[3]

This situation is a concern of society as a whole, and not simply of the workers involved, as the free market economists would argue, if we consider the nature of the activities in which the discouraged workers engage when they leave the market. Most economists misinterpret these workers' incentives and assume that they either go to school and continue their education or stay at home and help raise their families. While this may be true for middle-income discouraged workers, it is not true for many workers below the poverty threshold. They simply cannot afford to engage in either of these activities. No breadwinner with a spouse and two children who earns $1.63 an hour (or even $2.32 an hour) and who has no savings is in a position to continue his or her education. Even if he or she did, a diploma would do little good; Harrison has recently estimated that its value for a black ghetto resident over a 40-year working life is $6,000, or about $150 a year.[4] We must ask to what these added lifetime benefits should be contrasted to find out if such schooling is economically advantageous. The typical economist's response is the wages foregone when the person quits work and goes to school. Using any discount rate, a worker working at a wage of $1.63 an hour (or an annual salary of $3,260) who had to give up two years of work to go back to school would not find the investment worthwhile (even if we overlook the fact that there is no capital market where he could borrow such funds). But this is not the relevant cost that low-skilled workers bear when they quit work and go to school. In economic terms, such workers sacrifice the income they could have earned at their next best opportunity—their opportunity cost. For low-skilled workers this may not be the $1.63 an hour that we calculated before, but rather the wage they could have earned if they entered the crime industry, even when that wage is discounted by the high risk attached to such an occupation. Hence, for low-skilled workers the decisions faced are not between work and school or between labor-market work and housework, but rather among work, school, housework, welfare, and crime. Our high crime rate makes this empirically clear. For some workers, the rational choice is crime when all the relevant rates of return and risks are calculated.

One cannot analyze the market for low-skilled workers the way one analyzes the market for wheat or corn. If the equilibrium price of wheat or corn is low, little of it will be produced and the discouraged wheat or corn producers will take their resources and employ them *productively* in their next best opportunity—growing barley, say. Discouraged workers, however, especially low-skilled, low-income workers, may not take their resources—principally, their labor time—and employ all of them in a socially productive manner, but rather allocate some of them to socially destructive ends. Hence, there is a social cost (crime) to low equilibrium wages that is not captured by the market and consequently creates a mis-

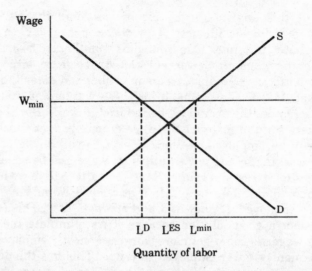

Figure 5–3. Equilibrium wage with a minimum-wage floor

taken market signal. In short, low wages themselves generate an externality, crime, that may be a *rational* response to the set of market wages. This externality is ignored by the free market analysis of these markets.

At this point the question of the minimum wage enters. Opponents of the minimum wage argue that it is a cause of teenage unemployment, which is a primary cause of teenage crime—"The devil finds work for idle hands." We can see this in Figure 5–3, which is identical to Figure 5–2 except for the inclusion of a minimum-wage floor W^{min}. The minimum wage prevents the market from working the way it naturally would by setting a wage of W^{ES} and employing L^{ES}. Instead, although L^{min} workers are willing to work at W_{min}, because it is so high only L^D are hired. The result of the minimum wage is to reduce the number of workers who find jobs from L^{ES} to L^D. Hence, $(L^{ES} - L^D)$ workers are idled by the minimum wage and, as the argument goes, are potential candidates for careers in crime.

But this analysis is myopic in assuming that the only cause of crime is idleness. Low wages can also be a main contributor to crime. This is obvious from Figure 5–3. At the minimum wage, L^{min} workers would decide to forgo their other options (including careers in crime) and enter the labor market. If sufficient demand for these workers at this wage were created, they could all be induced to work. But the laissez-faire solution is to let the wage drop to W^{ES}, at which only L^{ES} will be employed, while $(L^{min} - L^{ES})$ will be discouraged from working by the low equilibrium wage and be prime candidates for careers in crime. Hence one alternative we have is to impose a minimum wage. In that case we would have fewer people employed, L^D, but at a higher wage, W^{min}. This is obviously not a good solution because if we eliminate the minimum wage we could get more workers honestly employed and consequently fewer employed in crime. This has the dual effect of giving more people jobs and also of decreasing the crime rate. The minimum wage can simply not be justified in terms of our argument here. The second alternative is simply to let the wage fall to W^{ES}, the free market wage. This would employ L^{ES} workers, eliminate the crime previously committed under the minimum wage, and thereby increase society's welfare. This fact furnishes the basis for the free market argument on this point.

Although eliminating the minimum wage may be better than having it, the free market equilibrium is not optimal. There is a superior third alternative. This alternative is to eliminate the minimum wage but substitute a wage subsidy, either to employers or to employees, in its place. At the equilibrium wage rate W^{ES}, L^{ES} low-skilled workers offer their labor for honest employment and are employed. The rest are discouraged by a wage rate and are allocated to housework, school, or crime. The total cost of the crimes committed may be considerable if the equilibrium wage is very low. Therefore, anything we do to increase this equilibrium wage will reduce such crime costs by coaxing workers away from crime and into honest employment. This can be done by providing a wage subsidy to low-skilled workers or their employers. In order to determine the size of this subsidy, we must first determine how high we should try to make the new equilibrium wage. To do this, we merely need to resort to a simple utilitarian calculation. Each increase in the equilibrium wage rate cuts down on the crime rate and hence on the cost of crime. However, if we propose to increase the equilibrium wage by using a subsidy, every dollar increase in the equilibrium wage would cost the taxpayers money for the subsidy. The optimal equilibrium wage will be that wage at which the additional (or marginal) savings we get (through crime prevention) by raising the equilibrium wage rate one more dollar is exactly equal to the tax costs (subsidy) necessary to increase that equilibrium wage by that additional dollar. Let us call that optimal equilibrium wage W^{opt}. This situation is depicted in Figure 5–4.

In this figure we see our familiar supply and demand curves for labor denoted by S and D and the equilibrium wage W^{ES} that would exist in the unsubsidized labor market. At this wage rate a certain amount of crime exists in the economy. We have assumed that given the cost-benefit calculation

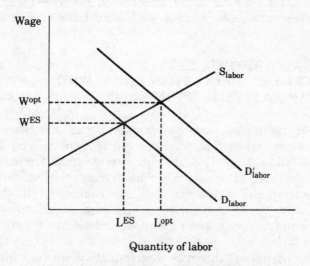

Figure 5–4. Equilibrium wage in a subsidized labor market

made above, the optimal equilibrium wage should be W^{opt}. The question is: How should we realize this optimal equilibrium? One way is to give a wage subsidy to employers of low-skilled labor, which would induce employers to hire more low-skilled workers at each market wage. In Figure 5–4 this would have the effect of shifting the labor demand curve to the right (see curve D'), which, if the subsidy is set correctly, would yield a subsidized market equilibrium wage at W^{opt}. This equilibrium is better than both the minimum-wage equilibrium and the free market equilibrium because, using our utilitarian calculations, it was worth paying the subsidy to reduce the crime rate.

The upshot of this discussion is that free market solutions may fail even when the good allocated seems to be a private good with no externalities (i.e., labor). The reason is rationality, although here the sequence of events is somewhat complicated. If it is rational for people to work honestly and hard when their honest wages are high, it may be just as rational for them to turn to antisocial forms of behavior when their honest wages are low. This rational response, however, actually creates an externality attached to low wages that must be taken into account when we design labor-market policy.

EQUAL OPPORTUNITY, ANTI-DISCRIMINATION LAWS, AND AFFIRMATIVE ACTION

One of the axioms stated in chapter 1 was that there is an unfortunate tradeoff between the efficiency of the free market system and the equity of the outcomes it can determine. However, for some situations this conflict may not exist. An excellent example of such a situation is considered by the statistical theory of discrimination, which justifies discriminatory hiring practices against minorities and women on efficiency grounds.

The statistical theory of discrimination emerges from the theory of markets with asymmetric information first studied by George Akerlof, which we have described in chapter 4.[5] The problem in these markets is that the agents on one side of the market are better informed about themselves than the agents on the other side. For instance, owners of used cars have better information about their products' quality than do the people shopping for them and, more important, owners of good cars have no way to signal to the buyers that their cars are good. The same is true for people wanting to borrow money or take out insurance—the whole market is tainted by the lemons.

The situation in the labor market is quite analogous. Workers appear at the personnel office and ask to be employed. The employer has no quick way to sort the efficient workers from the inefficient ones, and an extensive testing program may be prohibitively expensive. But there is more information available in the labor market than in the used-car market: employers can see whether applicants are old or young, male or female, and black or white. These broad statistical categories can be correlated with certain work-related characteristics and result in generalizations such as that old workers move less quickly than younger workers and that women have less steady employment records than men. Hence, an employer who does not wish to go to the expense of testing each worker and finding that the old worker runs around like a twenty-year-old, or that the young woman is totally committed to her career may, at the least cost, use external characteristics to guide his hiring. This employer will always take a man over a woman when their skills are equal since, statistically, the man will stay on the job longer and not interrupt his career to raise children. Hence, the high cost of testing each worker individually causes the employer to correlate his hiring to observable characteristics. According to the free market theory, this practice, although unfair, is economically sound, because it maximizes profits and the firm has no other obligation to society (remember the invisible-hand laissez-faire faith assumption). Thomas Sowell states the problem in terms of the costs of sorting and labeling people as follows:

Most objections to sorting and labeling in general—and particularly to the sorting and labeling of people—are based on ignoring the costs of knowledge, or ignoring differences in the cost of knowledge between one decision making process and another. Even objections on purely moral grounds to "discrimination" against various groups often turn out to involve ignoring knowledge costs. When an individual from a different group with a certain behavior pattern has a very different behavior pattern himself, judging him according to the group pattern, and making decisions accordingly, may impose serious costs on that individual. It also imposes costs (foregone opportunities) on the other person who made the incorrect assessment—and therefore provides an incentive for seeking alternative methods of assessment, if such are available at a cost commensurate with the benefit. However, insofar as the factual basis of the group assessment is accurate, the only costs paid by the group as a whole are costs created by its own behavior.

Those group members who do not in fact create such costs may pay a high price for being in the same category with others who do—and the cost-creators in turn pay correspondingly less than the costs created by their own behavior. It might be desirable from a moral or political point of view that public policy diffuse those costs over the general population rather than leave them concentrated on blameless individuals in the same category. That is a question of policy which depends on more variables than those being considered here. For the present analysis, the point is that group discrimination—costs imposed by group A as a whole on group B as a whole—is not proved by showing (in retrospect) that individuals of identical relevant characteristics are treated differently (in prospect) when they come from group A rather than group B. The two individuals may have identical probabilities of repaying credit, abstaining from violence, being a considerate neighbor, and contributing intelligent ideas. But only God can know that in advance free of charge. The cost of knowledge of these individuals' characteristics may be very different when the individual comes from group A than from group B, if these two groups as a whole differ in any of these characteristics.[6]

This practice appears manifestly unfair, especially to workers who are old, black, or female. There are many women who, if given the chance, would be willing to make the same personal sacrifices that men do to keep their jobs, just as there are many energetic older people who are fine workers. Why discriminate against them? The free market answer is an efficiency answer justified in utilitarian terms. It is clear that the increased output that we would get by finding the occasional worker who is the exception to the rule in these groups is small relative to the costs of finding such a person. Hence, it just does not pay to put our resources into the effort. While the system does not appear to be fair, the answer would go, it is at least efficient and we must always choose between efficiency and equity when we make social policy.

However in a wide variety of cases the equity-efficiency tradeoffs discussed above simply do not exist. Consider the following example. Two fraternal twins are born, one with red hair and one with brown hair. They grow up in the same family, go to the same school, and are inculcated with the same values of work and responsibility. The redhead, however, has very delicate hands and would make an excellent brain surgeon, while his brown-haired brother has great oratorical skills and would make an excellent lawyer. Consequently, society would best be served if the redhead were allocated to the medical profession and the brunette to the legal profession. Assume that doctors make more money than lawyers, so that both brothers wish to go to medical school, but only one spot exists. Depending upon the allocation of these twins, society's amount of medical and legal services will differ. If the redhead became a doctor, he would provide $500,000 worth of medical service; if he became a lawyer he would provide only $200,000 worth of legal services. Likewise, if the brunette were a doctor he would provide only $200,000 of medical services, while as a lawyer he would provide $500,000 of service. Hence, we can see that the most efficient allocation is to have the redhead become a doctor and the brunette a lawyer, thereby producing $1,000,000 worth of services to society.

Now we all know that pre-medical training is time-consuming and costly. Hence, the redhead is not likely to undertake such training unless he feels that he has a fair chance at being admitted to medical school. But let us say that both law schools and medical schools have learned that redheads, on the average, make terrible doctors but good lawyers, while brunettes make good doctors but bad lawyers. Hence, medical schools tend to reject candidates with red hair and accept candidates with brown hair, and law schools tend to do the opposite. Knowing this, our redhead will realize that, despite his good hands, the medical school will most likely accept his brother and reject him. Hence, he will not incur the cost of investing in pre-medical training because he knows, given his probability of acceptance, that the expected costs of such training will outweigh the benefits. Hence, he will apply to law school, his brother will apply to medical school, and society will get a suboptimal allocation of twins to professions, with the total value of the services created being $400,000 instead of $1,000,000.

Now, what would happen if a law were passed prohibiting this type of discrimination and that law schools and medical schools had to consider each applicant separately without respect to any extrinsic characteristic such as hair color?[7] First, this change would be costly. Each law school and medical school would have to set up a special testing program to find those rare redheaded applicants that would make good doctors. But, more important, redheads would take pre-medical courses in college because they would now know that if they are given a fair examination, their probability of success will be sufficiently high so as to justify their pre-medical investment. The result would be that if the testing equipment were efficient, a new allocation of twins to professions would result that would be socially optimal. The values of the services rendered by this allocation would be increased from $400,000 to $1,000,000 and, consequently, if the cost of the testing was less than $600,000, it would be both *fair* and *efficient* for society to institute such antidiscrimination laws in the legal and medical professions. The same argument can be made for affirmative action and quota rules, since the existence of these rules affects the incentives that gifted children of any group have to strive for advancement when they are young and such decisions will affect them throughout their lives.

Contrary to many free market arguments, we need not

always make a tradeoff between equity and efficiency, but rather in many situations *fairness may itself be the efficient way to proceed.* The preceding example showed that equity of the admissions system to law and medical school had allocative effects in that it influenced who in society made the effort to train themselves for such professions. Hence, if admissions are fair and known to be so, the best candidates will apply and efficiency will be increased.

EDUCATIONAL VOUCHERS

One of the most intriguing and popular free market proposals is for a system of educational vouchers that would replace the system of public schools as we know it today. This proposal, which was originally made by Milton Friedman, has caused great consternation among educators. The reason the proposal is seriously considered after nearly 20 years of debate is that it has not met with a convincing counterargument. This fact is quite remarkable since the educational voucher system represents a glaring inconsistency in free market economic thinking.

The educational voucher plan calls for the government to give all parents a voucher worth the cost of a public-school education. Parents can send their child to the private or public school of their choice by handing the voucher plus any additional tuition monies required to the school. The state would then reimburse the school for the value of the voucher. The result, according to Friedman, is that parents will send their children to the kind of school they want, whether progressive, conventional, or religious. Those schools that do not perform well will not be profitable and will fail, while those that perform well will flourish. The market will sort out the good and bad schools.

This plan appears to be the perfect free market proposal. First of all, it is individualistic, since each family is free to choose for itself where it will send its children, without state intervention. It is also a voluntaristic plan, since people can choose where to send their children. Finally, it should yield efficient outcomes, because schools that do not meet the individual needs of the student population are weeded out, and schools that do, remain.

The traditional arguments against the voucher system are based on arguments of equity and discrimination. I would like to play the devil's advocate and concentrate on other questions: Why should the government subsidize education at all? Why not eliminate public schools and subsidies to parents and institute an unsubsidized educational system? The answer that free market advocates would give (and grudgingly) is that education is a special commodity. It has positive externalities attached to it in that the value of educating an individual is worth more to society as a whole than it is to the individual himself. For instance, an educated person makes an educated voter. Such a voter helps to guarantee society that the best possible politicians get elected to office and to keep democracy sound. This is a benefit that all society receives and that is external to the individuals involved. If left alone individuals may not educate themselves up to the societally optimal level. Society pays for the benefit it gets with the voucher.

However, many other goods also possess externalities, some positive and some negative. For instance, health is a commodity that has external effects. Preventing a worker in a plant from getting a cold or contracting a contagious disease like polio not only gives him the benefit of the extra days' pay he would have to forgo if he reported sick, but also bestows benefits on his fellow workers whom he does not infect. It is curious then that free market advocates have not argued for a voucher system of, say, $2,000 a person a year to help Americans pay for their health care, which would be a logical extension of their arguments concerning education. If we had a system of national health care comparable to our system of public education, we would hear clamoring for a system of health vouchers as well. If the education voucher system is so beneficial, why not extend it to health care? The reason is that in the case of education it is convenient for free market advocates to propose state subsidies because they are a vehicle to eliminate an existing state-run program. But since there is no current state-run health system, free market advocates see no reason to extend their voucher system to it. In short, the benefit from vouchers is not its educational but its ideological merit—it replaces a state-run institution with a state-subsidized market institution. This is a definite plus as far as the individualistic free market argument is concerned.

Pursuing the issue, we can ask, Why doesn't the state use vouchers to subsidize the clothes, shelter, and food that citizens buy? The free market answer is that these goods do not carry externalities. If my roof leaks, I alone get wet. If my child is hungry, only he or she is affected. Hence, the argument goes, these things may be unfortunate, but they do not affect society at large and there is no obligation for the state to intervene. But this argument is myopic. If a portion of the population, however large, are corner dwellers and hence awarded near or below subsistence wages by the efficient market solution, they will not have the income to provide themselves and their families with food, clothing, and shelter. One rational response by corner dwellers to this state of affairs, as we saw earlier, is to allocate an increased portion of their time to illegal activities. Hence, if these goods are not subsidized, there will be an externality—crime. If a person with no market options is hungry, he may be forced to obtain food in non-market ways. The failure to subsidize these necessities for corner dwellers in the population carries with it externalities. Our cities are suffering today because middle-class inhabitants fear to go out in them at night. Workers are forced to commute hours from suburbs to center-city jobs because they are afraid to bring up their children in communities closer to the city. Suburban homeowners spend large sums of money on burglar alarms to protect their property. All these conditions are intimately related to the fact that a portion of the population is given a near-subsistence market wage and responds rationally to that wage. There are just as many externalities attached to not subsidizing food, shelter, and clothing as there are to not subsidizing education. The justification for these subsidies is then totally analogous to Friedman's justification for educational vouchers.

Consequently, the free market advocates box themselves into a corner when they advocate educational subsidies. If they subsidize education they cannot *logically* refuse to subsidize a variety of other goods, which they would steadfastly refuse to do. If they eliminated public education without a subsidy, they would surely ruin the educational system in the United States.

NOTES

1. Alfred Zucker, "Minimum Wages and the Long Run Demand for Low Wage Labor," *Quarterly Journal of Economics,* May 1973, pp. 267–272.
2. See "Resurgence of Sweatshops Reported in New York," *New York Times,* Thursday, Feb. 26, 1981, which states that the wage paid for sweatshop labor in New York was $1.50 per hour for a 50-hour week. Although we would expect this wage to be artificially low because some of these workers are illegal aliens, it must also be realized that in real terms this wage is lower than it appears because of the high cost of living in New York.
3. The estimate that there were 22.6 million people below the poverty level in 1976 can be found in *The Economic Report of the President,* Government Printing Office, Washington, D.C., 1982, p. 264. The other statistics stated in this and the preceeding paragraph are from Sar Levitan and Richard Belous, *More Than Subsistence: Minimum Wage for the Working Poor,* Baltimore: Johns Hopkins University Press, 1979.
4. Bennet Harrison, "Education and Unemployment in the Urban Ghetto," *American Economic Review,* 62(5), 1972, pp. 796–812.
5. George Akerlof, "The Market for Lemons: Quality, Uncertainty and Market Mechanism," *Quarterly Journal of Economics,* August 1970, pp. 488–500.
6. Thomas Sowell, *Knowledge and Decisions,* New York: Basic Books, 1981.
7. The *Equal Employment Opportunity Act of 1964* does not require any such testing procedure. All Title VII says is that it is not "an unlawful employment practice for an employer to give and to act upon the results of any professionally developed ability test provided that such test . . . is not designed, intended, or used to discriminate because of race, color, religion, sex or national origin." U.S. Code, Volume 42, Section 20000-2h. Hence, the legislation discussed in the chapter is, at the moment, non-existent but certainly feasible.

6

Free Market Assumptions: Some Experimental Evidence[1]

In recent years the economics profession has undergone a virtual revolution in the tools it uses to investigate economic hypotheses. Stimulated by the works of Vernon Smith and Charles Plott, economists have begun performing a wide variety of economic experiments whose purpose it is to study the predictive content of economic theories and the performance characteristics of proposed allocating institutions.

In these experiments paid human subjects are brought into a laboratory and asked to participate in a decision-making experiment that replicates the condition existing in naturally occurring markets or in recognized economic theories. The results of these experiments, after replication by other investigators, may serve as a guide in designing market institutions.

While the agenda of experimental economics has not been to test the assumptions made by the free market argument or its psychological and philosophic underpinnings as outlined in chapter 1, one can pick and choose some articles as shedding evidence on the validity of the free market assertions. In this chapter I wish to do just that. Basically I will return to three of the six characteristics of the argument (namely the equity-efficiency tradeoff, process orientation, and rationality and selfishness) and see whether, in a market-like context, these characteristics function as economists expect them to.

Each characteristic will be illustrated by an experiment which exemplifies it.

What we find is that while the market functions reasonably well and approximately the way we expect it to, the number of times our predictions are violated is sufficient to at least question the foundation upon which some of the free market argument is based. Let us investigate this more closely.

THE EQUITY-EFFICIENCY TRADEOFF: AFFIRMATIVE ACTION AND EQUAL OPPORTUNITY LAWS[2]

In the public policy debate surrounding the question of equal opportunity laws and affirmative action programs, there is a commonly held belief that a sad tradeoff exists between what is considered equitable and what is efficient. For example, it is felt that since corporations must sacrifice performance when they institute an affirmative action program, they are forced to pay for their "good intentions" with decreased corporate profits. If this were the case, we would not expect corporations to be eager to initiate such programs, especially since one of the tenets of the free market is the idea that corporations should not mix socially noble goals with their mandate to maximize the value of their shareholders' wealth. Adam Smith's faith in the free market stems from just this separation of goals, as our laissez-faire faith assumption of chapter 1 implies.

In a series of economic experiments recently performed at New York University by Clive Bull, Andrew Schotter, and Keith Weigelt, they have come to believe that in many empirically significant circumstances this supposed tradeoff between equity and efficiency simply does not exist.[3] In short, they find that what is equitable may also be efficient. More precisely, in terms of equal opportunity laws their experiments indicate that the imposition of such laws increases the incomes of disadvantaged groups and unambiguously increases the profits of the corporation instituting them. The reason for this is simple. If previously discriminated against groups are suddenly treated like equals, they have an incentive to try harder. If they try harder, they will elicit more effort from their previously advantaged colleagues. Hence, since all agents in the organization are trying harder, corporate output will increase without the firm's incurring any extra costs. In short, corporate profits rise. The results concerning affirmative action laws are more complex. If the amount of historical discrimination in the corporation or society is not great, their results indicate that while such programs do increase the probability that disadvantaged groups get promoted, they tend to reduce the output and hence profitability of the organization. However, if an affirmative action program is instituted in a situation in which some groups have met with a great deal of historical discrimination, not only do these programs help the disadvantaged group but they also increase the profits of the firms instituting them.

The reason for these results is again straightforward. When a group is highly discriminated against, group members tend to become discouraged and "drop out" (i.e., they exert no effort). When an affirmative action program is instituted, these people start to try since they realize the "playing field" is more level and they have an opportunity for promotion and the other perks of career advancement. As in the case of equal opportunity laws, these increased effort levels spur advantaged agents to try harder themselves, with similar results for corporate profits.

When the amount of historical discrimination is not as great, their results differ because, under these circumstances, agents discriminated against never drop out. They try at least a little. Hence, when the affirmative action program is implemented, they take their newly awarded preferential status as an opportunity to coast since, with the same effort as before, they will now be promoted and advanced with greater probability. Their diminished efforts induce their colleagues to do so as well, and corporate profits and output fall.

To properly understand the Bull, Schotter, and Weigelt experiments, we must first describe how they characterize the problem of affirmative action and equal opportunity laws. In short, they view economic organizations as presenting agents with a set of tournaments in which they compete for prizes. Tournaments differ from other incentive schemes in that an agent's payment in a tournament depends only on his performance relative to that of others with whom he is compared. In a two-person tournament, the performance of one agent is compared with the performance of another. On the basis of this comparison, the high-performance agent receives a higher payment relative to that of the low-performance agent.

A firm's hierarchical structure inherently contains characteristics of rank order tournaments: as the organizational pyramid narrows, only the top-ranked agents move to the next, and smaller, set of promotions. For example, in corporations, several vice-presidents may compete to be promoted to the presidency. In universities, untenured assistance professors compete with each other to get one of a limited number of tenured slots. In car dealerships, salesmen compete to see who can sell the most cars. The one who does is given a bonus. When all people are identical and compete in fair or symmetrical tournaments, the theory of such tournaments predicts that all people will supply equal amounts of effort (i.e., they will try equally hard) and chance will determine who gets ahead.

A tournament can be asymmetrical in two ways. It can be uneven when it is more costly for some people to perform than others. For example, if one group in society has been discriminated against in the past, one can assume that they have been deprived of some of the educational opportunities that other groups had. Hence, it may be more arduous for them to function in similar jobs than for others who have not been the victims of such discrimination. A tournament can also be unfair. In such tournaments, people are identical in the sense of having the same cost of effort, but the rules of the organization are skewed against them. That is, they are discriminated against. For example, if a tournament is unfair, some agents, in order to be promoted, not only have to perform better but must perform substantially better.

Bull, Schotter, and Weigelt consider affirmative action programs as attempts to compensate groups for their high cost of effort by changing the rules of the tournament to favor them. In short, affirmative action programs take uneven but fair tournaments and make them uneven and unfair tournaments by treating previously discriminated groups preferentially. Equal opportunity laws take unfair tournaments and make them fair.

Before we describe the particular experiment performed, it is important to explain why an experiment on this topic might be important. In recent years experiments have become accepted as a useful and legitimate way to test economic theories. The control of the laboratory also allows the testing of allocation and incentive mechanisms for which naturally occurring field data do not exist. In short, experiments are a cheap way to pretest corporate allocating and incentive schemes before they are implemented by the corporation (i.e., before the point at which mistakes become costly).

Given the present characterization of affirmative action programs and equal opportunity laws, it is not surprising that Bull, Schotter, and Weigelt tested the performance of economic tournaments in their symmetrical, unfair, and uneven forms. A typical experiment was conducted as follows. First a group of students, usually 24, from economics courses at New York University, were recruited. They reported to a room that had chairs placed around its perimeter, each chair facing the wall. The students were randomly assigned seats and subject numbers, and given written instructions.

Each subject was informed that another subject was randomly assigned as his or her "pair member" and that the amount of money he or she would earn in the experiment was a function of his or her decisions, his or her pair member's decisions, and the realizations of a random variable. The physical identity of the pair member was not revealed. The experiment then began. Each subject was then asked to choose an integer between 0 and 100. This was called his or her "decision number," and each subject entered his or her choice on the worksheet. Corresponding to each decision number was a cost listed in a table in the instructions. The larger the number chosen, the greater the associated cost. After subjects recorded their decision numbers, and experimental administrator circulated with a box containing bingo balls labeled with the integers, including zero, usually from -40 to $+40$. These were called "random numbers." Each subject would pull a random number from the box, replace it, enter it on his or her worksheet, then add it to the decision number to yield the "total number" for that round. This information was recorded on a slip of paper, which was then collected from the subject. An administrator compared the total numbers of each pair of subjects. He then announced which pair member had the highest total number in each pair. The pair members with the highest and lowest total numbers were awarded respectively, "fixed payments" M and m, $M > m$. Each subject then calculated his or her payoff for the round by subtracting the cost of his or her decision number from the fixed payment. All the tournaments parameters except the identity of each subject's pair member were known to all subjects.

When this round was completed and the payoffs were recorded, the next round began. All the rounds were identical. Each group of subjects repeated this procedure for 20 rounds. When the last round was completed, the subjects calculated their payoffs for the entire experiment by adding up their payoffs for the 20 rounds and subtracting $2. The experiments lasted approximately 75 minutes, and subjects earned between $5 and $13. These incentives seemed to be more than adequate.

Note the strategic nature of the experiment. Subjects knew that their earnings depended on their actions (their decision number or their "level of effort") and the actions (decision numbers or effort levels) of their pair member. Subjects had to ponder the following tradeoff: the more effort they expended, the more likely they would receive the high fixed payment, but also the higher were the associated costs of effort that would be subtracted from their fixed payments. Note finally that luck (the random number) plays a role in the experiment as well.

Unfair tournaments changed the rules of the experiment by defining a parameter which told subjects by how much the output of disadvantaged subjects had to exceed the outputs of their advantaged counterparts in order that they should receive the high fixed payment.

Seven experiments were conducted. Experiment 1 was symmetrical in terms of both the costs of the subject and the rules of the experimental tournament. Experiments 2 and 3 investigated how unfairness affects the behavior of subjects by asking them to go through the same procedure as in experiment 1 but specifying that one group of subjects had outputs that were, respectively, 25 and 45 units greater than their advantaged counterparts in order to win. Experiments 4 and 5 investigated the impact of unevenness in tournaments by specifying that one set of subjects had cost of efforts which were respectively twice (experiment 4) and four times (experiment 5) that of their counterparts. Finally, experiments 6 and 7 present our laboratory version of affirmative action programs. In experiment 6(7) we take the parameters of experiment 4 where one subject's cost of effort is twice the other, introducing a rule of asymmetry which favors the other, and introducing a rule of asymmetry which favors the other subject by allowing him to obtain the big payment of M even if his total number was 25(45) units below that of his cost-advantaged foe. The effect of equal opportunity laws can be investigated by comparing the results of experiments 2 and 3 with the results of experiment 1 since those pair-wise comparisons would demonstrate the effects of making previously unfair tournaments fair.

The impact of affirmative action programs is investigated by comparing the results of experiments 6 and 7 with the results of experiments 4 and 5 since, in these cases (experiments 6 and 7), previously uneven but fair tournaments (experiments 4 and 5) are transformed into uneven and unfair tournaments in a way that compensates previously cost-disadvantaged groups with a rules advantage.

TOURNAMENT RESULTS

In general, the theory of tournaments predicts subjects' behavior fairly well. On average, subjects supplied the amount of effort predicted by the theory. In a separate set of experiments, Bull, Schotter, and Weigelt showed that as parameters changed, subjects revised their behavior as predicted by the theory.[4]

As predicted, subjects react differently to the type of asymmetry.

In unfair tournaments, (in which the rules discriminate against one set of agents), the theory predicts that despite the level of discrimination, all agents will choose the same effort level. Additionally, the theory predicts that as the level of discrimination increases, agents will decrease their amount of effort. The authors found that in their experiments the behavior of subjects conformed to these predictions.

In uneven tournaments (tournaments in which one set of agents finds it more costly to perform a task), the theory predicts that the different types of agent will choose different effort levels and that the difference in their effort level is equal to the differential in their cost of effort. For example, an agent who has a cost of effort that is twice as high as another agent's will only supply half the effort (because effort is twice as costly to him). Their results show that in uneven tournaments subjects did behave as predicted.

Equal opportunity laws were quite effective in increasing the effort levels of discriminated against group members. This increase in effort causes discriminated against group members to realize greater savings. The laws also increase the effort levels of advantaged subjects; thus the net effect is that these laws increased the tournament's total effort. These findings suggest that equal opportunity laws not only help discriminated against group members but also increase the output and hence the profits of the firm. Strategically, this finding suggests that it is in the firm's best interest not to allow discrimination in the workplace.

Affirmative action programs always increase the earnings of discriminated against group members. When the degree of cost disadvantageousness is low between high- and low-ability agents, these programs tend to reduce the effort levels of *all* subjects, so the total tournament output is reduced. However, when the degree of cost disadvantageousness is high, affirmative action programs tend to increase the effort levels of all subjects, hence the tournament's total output increases.

We can draw the following implications. Not only do affirmative action programs always increase the earnings of agents with high costs of effort but, when the degree of disadvantageousness is high enough, the programs can actually increase the output of the firm. Hence, the often discussed tradeoff between equity and efficiency may not be operative in the case of equal opportunity laws and affirmative action programs (or at least our laboratory version of them) where high levels of historical discrimination exist. Equity may actually be a necessary condition for efficiency.

RATIONALITY, SELFISHNESS AND PROCESS ORIENTATION[5]

If the free market agents are rational and selfish then they should not care about the satisfaction of others in evaluating market outcomes. Hence, when given a choice between decision 1, which gives agents more money and other people less, and decision 2, which would have the opposite effect, decision 1 should always be chosen. An extremely interesting experiment by Elizabeth Hoffman and Mathew Spitzer throws some doubt on this proposition and upon the selfishness assumption of free-market economics.[6] Let us investigate their experiment.

The Hoffman–Spitzer experiment

The Hoffman–Spitzer experiment that we will describe was inspired by an earlier experiment by the same authors.[7] That experiment attempted to investigate the predictions of the famous Coase theorem mentioned earlier in chapter 4. The tests involved in that experiment were as follows (for brevity we will discuss the two-person full information version of the experiment only).

Two subjects were brought into a room. A coin was then flipped to designate one of them as the "controller." The subjects were then given a sheet of paper with the following table on it.

| | Problem 1 | | | Problem 2 | |
| | Participant | | | Participant | |
Number	A	C	Number	A	B
0	$0.00	$12.00	0	$0.00	$11.00
1	4.00	10.00	1	1.00	10.00
2	6.00	6.00	2	2.00	8.00
3	8.00	4.00	3	4.00	6.00
4	9.00	2.00	4	5.50	5.50
5	10.00	1.00	5	9.00	4.00
6	11.00	0.00	6	10.50	1.00

Subjects were told that they would engage in two decision problems in sequence with the designated controller for the second problem being chosen after the first was completed.

Looking at problem 1 we see three columns of numbers. Column 1 simply indicates the row of the table we are looking at and runs from 0 to 6. In each row there are two numbers indicating the payoff to the two subjects labeled A and B. If subject A is designated the controller then he can do one of two things. He can either choose a row and determine payoff indicated there for himself and the other, or he can agree with the partner to choose a row and then bargain over how joint payoffs indicated in that row will be split (side payments between the subjects are allowed). Note the choice for the controller. If he wanted he could choose row 6 and get $11 for himself and give $0 to the partner. The *joint* payoff to both would then be $11. However, a choice of row 1 gives the two of them $14 to split so that there is enough money to make both of them better off than with the controller's unilateral choice of row 6. All they have to do is agree on how to split the $14. Rationality and selfishness would indicate that the designated controller would never agree to a split of the $14 giving him less than $11 since he could unilaterally give himself that much simply by choosing row 6. Any split which is worse for him would not be individually rational. What Hoffman and Spitzer found, however, was that controllers tended to share the $14 gain available to the two of them and accepted less than their $11 security level. In fact 18 of the 20 controllers in the two-person experiment split the $14 equally between themselves and their partners, each taking $7. Such a result seems to violate the precepts of rationality and selfishness upon which the free market argument rests.

Faced with these surprising results Hoffman and Spitzer attempted to investigate why such seemingly irrational behavior arose. It was their hypothesis that, even though the controller was "entitled" by the experimental administrator to grab at least $11 for himself, students did not feel that that entitlement constituted a "right" since the designation "controller" was arbitrarily determined. In our terminology, subjects cared about *the process* determining eventual payoffs as well as the payoffs themselves.

To capture this concern with process Hoffman and Spitzer hypothesized that the reason why controllers, who were arbitrarily assigned, failed to exercise their strategic prerogatives and get at least $11 for themselves was that they felt they had not *earned* the right to keep $11. Hence in the Hoffman–Spitzer 1985 experiment, subjects were presented with a two-stage game. In stage 1 they played a game called "nim." The "winner" of this game was then said to have "earned" the right to be controller in a game similar to the one just discussed. The conjecture of Hoffman and Spitzer was that subjects entertained a Lockean view of justice (see Chapter 1) which asserts that economic agents have the right to keep anything they earn (or mix their labor with). Thus, if they earned the right to be controller they would feel justified in keeping a more than equal share of the proceeds received through cooperation.

In fact, this is what they found. In the experiments where subjects played nim and were told the winner "earned" the right to be controller, more than half of the splits gave the controller more than their individual (unilateral) maximum. Only 22 percent were within $1.00 of the equal split. In experiments where subjects were merely designated controller, 73 percent of the decisions were nearly equal splits.

One is led to conclude from these experiments that, in isolation, the precepts of rationality and selfishness upon which the free market argument is based are not enough to explain the behavior of economic agents. One must also include some process theory which will allow economic agents to act selfishly. Clearly, the Lockean theory is one which does this and does it convincingly, but one wonders how culturally based this underlying theory is. For example, in societies where individualism is not so highly cherished and hence where the Lockean theory has less sway (say in Japan) we would not expect the same results. For example, as Hoffman and Spitzer point out, if this experiment were run on a set of doctrinaire Marxists, we would expect that the available money might be split according to some perceptions of people's needs as opposed to their strategic capabilities. This all leads us to wonder whether a cross-national or (cross-cultural) study of this phenomenon would yield different results.

FREE-RIDING[8]

In chapter 4 we agreed that the free market may fail when it attempts to allocate what are called "public goods" since the proper allocation of these goods relies on individuals truthfully revealing how much they are willing to pay to have such goods provided and such truth-telling behavior may not be forthcoming from rational selfish agents. However it is one thing to theorize about such free-riding behavior and another to actually attempt to measure how serious a problem free-riding might in fact be. Many phenomena look serious on the blackboard only to prove innocuous empirically in the real world. For experimental economics there is a real advantage in studying phenomena like free-riding since it allows the investigator to induce and control the value that subjects place on hypothetical public goods. By then looking at the reported values submitted by these agents and comparing them with the values induced, we can measure the degree of misrepresentation or lying. Next we can change the mechanism or institution used to allocate these goods and see how such institutional changes affect the degree of misrepresentation.

Is Free-riding a Problem?

Early experimental investigations concerning free-riding implied that empirically it was not a problem. Early in the modern debate about free-riding, Lief Johansen stated "I do not know of many historical results or other empirical evidence which show convincingly that the problem of correct revelation or preferences has any practical significance."[9] A review of the free-riding experimental literature by Al Roth refers to an early study by Peter Bohm sponsored by the Swedish Radio-T.V. broadcasting company.[10] In this experiment adult residents of Stockholm were asked to come for an interview for which they would be given a fee. They were asked how much of the fee they would be willing to pay to watch a program of two popular comedians. They were told that they would be shown the program only if the sum of contributions made by them and others interviewed was greater than the cost of showing it. However, once it was decided that it would be shown, all subjects could view it. There were five different rules used to inform subjects how much they would be charged if the show was seen. One rule charged them the amount they offered, one charged a percentage of that amount and one charged nothing at all, etc. Clearly these different rules led to different incentives to tell the truth. (Compare the rule where you are asked to pay the full amount you offer and the one where you pay nothing.) The fact that the subjects appeared to offer equal contributions no matter what rule was used was taken by Bohm as evidence that their intent was to tell the truth and not to take advantage of the free-riding possibilities. Bohm's experiment can be used as support for Johansens's statement that free-riding is not an empirically relevant problem. Other experiments, by Schneider and Pommerehne,[11] Marwell and Ames, and others, came to similar conclusions.

Most of these studies suffered from the fact that the experiments aimed to measure the willingness of subjects to pay for a public good (instead of controlling this willingness to pay in the laboratory) and were only performed once. Hence, subjects did not have the opportunity to learn that dishonesty might be the most profitable policy.

Isaac, McCue and Plott rectified this problem. They performed a set of experiments in which subjects were given schedules indicating how much the experimental administrator was willing to pay them for each unit of the public good produced. In short, they were given demand schedules for the good and their payoff was the difference between the value of the good produced and the amount they had to contribute to it. For example, let us say that subjects were told that if one unit of the public good was produced they would be paid $3, if two units they would be paid an additional $2, if three units were produced they would be paid yet another dollar. Each unit from the fourth on was worthless. If two units were produced and they were charged $1 per unit, their payoff would be the sum of their values on the first two units ($3 + $2) minus their contribution of $2, or $5 − $2 = $3. In the experiment, after receiving the valuation schedules, subjects would write their contributions on pieces of paper which were collected. An assumed constant marginal cost of $1.30 was used to determine the quantity of public good to produce (that quantity at which the marginal aggregate willingness to pay equalled $1.30) and people were then asked to pay what they wrote down on their papers as contributions. This experiment was repeated ten times.

What Isaac et al. found was that as time went on the amount the subjects were willing to contribute diminished and approached the zero contribution (the pure free-ride point), although it never got there. They also found that the first period contributions were distinctly different from the later contributions (they were higher) and that learning increased free-riding. Isaac et al. took this as an indication that repetition and learning were essential ingredients of the free-riding story. Since such repetition is a feature of real world public goods situations, we might interpret their results as a piece of evidence suggesting that the free-rider problem is alive and well in the outside world.

RATIONALITY: HONESTY AND INCOMPETENCY IN MARKETS WITH ASYMMETRIC INFORMATION[12]

As discussed in chapter 4, the very rationality that leads the market to efficiency may also lead it to fail when the market contains asymmetric information, public goods or externalities. In the mid 1980s, Pitchik and Schotter performed a set of experiments to see whether markets for expert diagnosis and care (markets with asymmetric information) function efficiently in the sense of creating the proper incentives for experts to offer truthful diagnoses to customers who solicit their opinion.[13] Another similar experiment was performed by Plott and Wilde.[14] What Pitchik and Schotter find is that although such markets (or at least their laboratory representations) do elicit significantly high honesty levels, there is still some room for government intervention, especially licensing programs, to help raise efficiency levels beyond those determined under laissez-faire.

To give a flavor of the way this particular experiment was performed, the instructions given to the subjects will be presented. Although this may be tedious, it is probably the best way to give the flavor of the experiment as well as describe its inner workings. After this the experimental design and the results will be presented.

PITCHIK AND SCHOTTER INSTRUCTIONS

The aim of this experiment is to investigate a number of hypotheses about the way people make decisions in situations where information is not complete. In the experiment some of you will play the role of an expert, whose job it will be to give diagnostic opinions to a set of consumers, while others will play the role of consumers (searchers) who will be trying to make a decision based on the information given by the experts. Consumers will be paid according to whether or not they make the right decision; experts will be paid according to the opinion they give and the opinions given by other experts. If you choose correctly during the experiment you will earn a nice payoff. The experiment will take approximately 1–1½ hours and you will be paid at the end.

The following instructions will explain the experiment in greater detail and explain also how your final payoff will be determined. After you read them we will discuss them and then have several practice rounds before we actually begin.

THE EXPERIMENT

This experiment examines the market for expert diagnosis and care. One such market might be the market for car repairs. In these markets a set of experts (car mechanics) diagnose and treat problems that a set of consumers (car owners) have. The consumers are assumed to be ignorant of the cause of their problem and consequently must search for opinions in order to help them decide. The problem for the consumers is that the experts may have an incentive to lie and recommend unnecessary repairs. Furthermore, in these markets some experts are incompetent and are capable of giving honest, but incorrect diagnoses. Hence, if you are a consumer searching for a correct repair you must take into account that some of the opinions you receive are correct, some are knowingly false while others are honestly but incompetently offered.

To capture the essence of this type of market we assigned six of you the role of experts and six of you the role of consumers. Which role you will have is indicated in the upper right-hand corner of your instruction sheet. Among the experts three are competent and three incompetent.

The market you will participate in will work as follows. Assume, for convenience, that the consumers are car owners each of whose car has broken down and that each car can either have a major problem or a minor problem. We will now explain the instructions for you if you've been assigned the role of the searcher.

THE SEARCHER

For the consumers we have arranged it so that three of you have major problems and three have minor problems. You will not be able to know which problem you have.

The price of the major repair will be 450 while the price of a minor repair will be 350. Your objective as a consumer is to solicit opinions as to what is wrong with your car and then to decide on whether you want a minor or major repair.

The firm's objective will be to make money from customers like you, by offering either honest or dishonest opinions. Remember, however, that the experts you get opinions from can either be honest and competent, honest and incompetent, or dishonest and incompetent.

A dishonest competent firm will look at your car, know, without doubt, what is wrong with your car, but then tell you that your problem is major and charge you 450. He will then do the minimum repair necessary to fix the car correctly and pocket the extra charge.

Incompetent stations differ from competent ones in that when they look at your car they will not be sure whether your car has a minor or major problem. In fact, we have designed it such that on any car they will know that their diagnosis is correct only 80 percent of the time. Honest incompetent firms will try to give you a correct opinion but may make a mistake while dishonest incompetent firms will always say major.

Hence, when you search for opinions, the opinion you get will depend upon the problem with your car and the expert you visit. The exact opinion you will get is portrayed in Table 6–1.

Notice that you can figure out what any type of firm will tell you about your car if you know your problem, except an honest incompe-

Table 6–1. Opinions offered by type of expert and type of car problem

	You are competent and acting honestly	*You are competent and acting dishonestly*	*You are in-competent and acting honestly*	*You are in-competent and acting dishonestly*
Car problem is minor	Opinion is minor	Opinion is major	Opinion is uncertain (could be major or minor)	Opinion is major
Car problem is major	Opinion is major	Opinion is major	Opinion is uncertain (could be major or minor)	Opinion is major

tent firm whose opinion is uncertain. Hence, if your car has a major problem you can still get a minor opinion on it from an honest incompetent firm, while if it is minor, you can get a major opinion as well. It all depends on whom you ask and remember that three experts are competent and three incompetent and that they will decide on their honesty–dishonesty levels.

Your job is to solicit opinions and then decide if you want to get a major or minor repair. The way you solicit opinions is simple. In front of you is a computer terminal. If you do not want an opinion but rather want to decide on a repair without searching, type the word NO into the terminal to answer the terminal's question "Do you want to search?" The terminal will then respond by asking you for your repair decision by writing: Major or Minor repair? You will then reply by typing either of the words MAJOR or MINOR, and your participation in this trial of the experiment will be over.

If you want one or more opinions before you decide on a repair all you need to do is type the word YES.

The computer will then pick one of the firms at random (each firm will be equally likely to be chosen) and generate an opinion according to the opinion rules chosen by the firms. Each time you search it will cost you some money (4 in this experiment). If after one search you are ready to make a decision, type NO when the terminal asks you if you want to search again and after its reply tell it your decision by typing either MINOR or MAJOR into the terminal. If you want another opinion simply type SEARCH again. You can search at most three times before you will have to make a decision.

Your payoff will be determined as follows: Before each trial we will credit your account with 650. Your final payoff will be 650 − (number of searches) × the cost of search − the price of repair. For example, say you search three times and decide to choose a major repair. Then your final payoff will be $188 = 650 - 3 \times 4 - 450$. It is assumed that a major repair will fix both a major and a minor problem, so that in this case your payoff will be simple. However, say you searched three times and decided to get a minor repair. If your car actually had a minor problem then you make the correct decision and your payoff would be $650 - 3 \times 4 - 350 = 288$, which is clearly better than the payoff you would have gotten if you had gotten a major repair. If your car actually had a major problem however, then you would have made the wrong decision and you car will still not be fixed. In this case we assume that you must pay the service station the cost of the minor repair 150 and then get it fixed as a major repair. Hence, your payoff here would be $38 = 650 - 3 \times 4 - (450 + 150)$, which is worse than both of the other payoffs.

Notice, that if you choose a major repair you may run the risk of paying 450 for a repair that should cost you only 350 if your problem were minor, while if you choose a minor repair you run the risk of having your problem turn out to be major in which case you will have to get it fixed twice at a total cost of $150 + 450$ instead of 450. No matter what your problem is then, you always will maximize your payoff by choosing the correct repair. (If you knew what that was.)

After all consumers have stopped searching and made their decisions, we will tell you your payoffs in this trial, and the average honesty/dishonesty configuration among the firms. The next trial will then begin. Three consumers will randomly be assigned major problems, three will be assigned minor problems. The experts will then be allowed to change the way they offer opinions and then we will repeat the experiment. This will occur ten times. Your final payoff will be the sum of monies you have collected in each of the ten periods.

EXPERTS

If subjects were experts the instructions would read as follows. You will make profits by giving opinions to the searchers. Notice that when you sat down at the computer, the terminal confirmed whether you are competent or incompetent. Given your competency, the opinion you give to any consumer who comes into the shop will be determined by whether you are acting honestly or dishonestly. For instance, if you are competent and decide to act honestly, you will look at the customer's car, know without doubt whether his car has a major problem, give him an honest opinion, and fix his car as you said you would (charging 450 if you said major and 350 if you said minor). If you act dishonestly, you would look at his car, know without doubt what is wrong with it, but then tell him that his problem is major and charge him 450. You would then do the minimum repair necessary to fix the car correctly. Incompetent stations differ from competent ones in that they will not be sure whether the car has a minor or major problem.

Competent Experts

If you are competent, your only decision will be whether or not to be honest or dishonest in offering opinions to consumers. However, you do not have to be honest or dishonest all the time, but rather you can choose to be honest any percent of the time between 0 percent and 100 percent. After you decide how often you want to be honest, simply type a number between 0 and 100 into your terminal after it asks you for this information. This number will indicate the portion of the time you want to be honest. Remember, the higher the fraction you choose, the more often or the greater the probability will be that you will give an honest opinion. The computer will then offer your opinions for you as you are chosen at random by the searchers.

To illustrate how your payoff will depend on your honesty/dishonesty choice, consider the following: Assume a car with a minor problem comes to you to get a repair. If you offer him a minor opinion (act honestly), you would fix his car with a minor repair and earn $200 = (350 - 150)$. If you act dishonestly, you would have offered him a major opinion and fixed the car with a minor repair. Your profits would be $300 = (450 - 150)$ in this case.

If a car with a major problem comes to you, you would offer a major opinion and fix the car as major (you have no other option). Hence your profits would be $200 = (450 - 250)$. This then tells you what your profits are *if* a car owner allows you to fix his car. As you see, they depend on your *your* opinion and your repair rule only. However, the *numbers* of cars you fix depends not only on your opinion, but on the opinion given by the other firms (since consumers are searching), and if they are different from yours, you run the risk of not being believed and getting only a few cars to fix.

To illustrate the tradeoffs existing here, let us say that a car owner with a minor problem comes into your service station for an opinion. Obviously, you will make the most profit from this car if you can have the owner return to you and buy a major repair, but fix the car with a minor procedure (your profit would be $(450 - 150)$). Hence you might be tempted to be dishonest and offer a major opinion. However, if all of the other firms are honest, then it is likely that this car owner will get some (if not many) minor opinions in his searching and may decide to get a minor repair, in which case you would make zero profit on his car. Consequently, there is a tradeoff in offering opinions. While dishonest opinions yield high profits on each minor problem car that returns to you to fix, the number of cars that actually come to you for repairs depends upon the opinions that the other firms offer, i.e. on the honesty/dishonesty configuration amongst the firms. If you are offering opinions way out of line with those of other firms, you are likely to get fewer customers (unless, of course, you are offering opinions which are consonant with the searcher's decisions).

To describe how your payoffs are calculated, say there is a searcher with a minor problem (he, of course, will be unaware of his true problem). As he searches, he will get opinions from the experts and eventually will stop and decide. Say he decides to get a major repair. If so, we will look at all the firms who would have given this car owner a major opinion if he asked them and divide his business up equally among them. For instance, only dishonest firms would offer a car owner with a minor problem a major opinion. If there are K such firms, each will get 1/K of this business and then make the profit on it described above. For instance, if you are competent and dishonest, you would be included in the pool of people who share this profit. You would fix the car with a minor repair and earn $(450 - 150)$ on it. Hence, your profit from this one car is $(1/K)(450 - 150)$. The same thing is done for car owners with minor problems who get minor repairs, car owners with major problems who get major repairs and car owners with major problems who get minor repairs.

So you can see that your honesty and opinions rules combined with those of all the other firms have a dual effect. They first of all determine which cars you will share the profits of and secondly, combined with your repair rule if you are incompetent, they determine how much profit you will make on each car you fix.

After every trial, we will tell you your final payoff, the average honesty/dishonesty mix among the competent and incompetent firms and the average payoff of the other firms of your competency. You will then be asked to repeat the experiment again and we will do this for ten trials. Your final payoff will be the sum of your ten trial payoffs and you will be paid at the end.

Incompetent Experts

As an incompetent expert, you will make profits by offering opinions and doing repairs. To do this, you will have to instruct the computer as to how you are going to behave by specifying an honesty rule, an opinion rule, and a repair rule. The terminal will ask you for this information in sequence.

The honesty rule simply tells the computer the percentage of the time you will act honestly when a searcher asks you for an opinion. To enter it, simply type a number between 0 and 100 into the terminal as it asks you for that information. This will specify your honesty percentage. Remember, a higher number means greater honesty.

The opinion and repair rules are used to instruct the computer how you want to behave during the time when you are being honest and dishonest. Remember that because you are incompetent, you will not know for sure what is wrong with any car that comes into your shop. If fact, you can assume that you have a diagnostic machine that is right only 80 per cent of the time. When you act dishonestly, no matter what your diagnostic machine signals, you will always offer a major opinion. However, when you are being honest, you will try to give a correct opinion (or the best opinion you can given the accuracy of your machine) and hence you can follow one of the following four rules:

1. Always offer a minor opinion.
2. Always offer the opposite opinion from what your diagnostic machine says.
3. Always offer the same opinion as your machine says.
4. Always say major.

Finally, when you are acting dishonestly, despite the fact that you always offer major opinions, you still have the option of repairing the cars with either a minor or a major repair. You might want to do the minimum repair necessary to fix the car, but since you are incompetent and do not know what is wrong with it, you will have to choose a repair decision that depends on what your diagnostic machine tells you. The four possible repair rules are listed below:

1. Always fix the car as minor.
2. Always fix the car in a manner opposite to the signal of your diagnostic machine (i.e., if the machine says the car has a major problem, fix it as minor).
3. Always fix the car in accordance with the signal of your diagnostic machine (i.e., if the machine says the car has a major problem, fix it as major).

4. Always fix it as major.

To choose a repair rule, simply type one of the numbers (1), (2), (3), or (4) into the terminal as you are asked. (If you choose always to be honest, you will not have to answer this question and your terminal will instruct you otherwise.)

Consequently, as incompetent experts, you will be asked by the terminal to specify three pieces of information:

1. An honesty fraction (a number between 0 and 100).
2. An opinion rule (either (1) or (2) or (3) or (4)).
3. A repair rule (either (1) or (2) or (3) or (4)).

To determine your payoff, we will have to make one simple assumption. It is that a major repair done on a car fixes both a major problem and a minor problem, while a minor repair fixes only a minor problem. Hence, let us say that a car with a major problem comes to you for an opinion and, using your opinion rule and the signal given by the diagnostic machine, you offer a major opinion. If that car owner, after getting other opinions, comes back to you and asks you to fix his car, you will earn a profit of $(450 - 250) = 200$, if your repair rule instructed you to do a major repair. However, if you offered a major opinion, but fixed the car with a minor repair, it would not be fixed and you will then have to fix it again at your own expense. Your payoff here will be $(450 - 150 - 250) = 50$. Consequently, if you are incompetent, you face a tradeoff: If a car returns to you for a repair, you make the most money if you offered a major opinion but performed a minor repair (assuming that that repair is correct). However, if you attempt this and are wrong, you will have to absorb the cost of your mistake and your profits will fall.

This then tells you what your profits are *if* a car owner allows you to fix his car. As you can see, they depend on *your* opinion and repair rule only. However, the *number* of cars you fix depends on not only your opinion but on the opinions given by the other firms (since consumers are searching) and if other opinions are different from yours, you run the risk of not being believed and getting only a few cars to fix.

To illustrate the tradeoffs existing here, let us say that a car owner with a minor problem comes into your service station. Obviously, you will profit most if you can convince the owner to buy a major repair and then fix the car with a minor procedure. (Your profit in this case would be $300 = (450 - 150)$.) Hence you will be tempted to be dishonest and offer a major opinion. However, if all of the other firms are honest, then it is likely that this car owner will get minor opinions in his searching and may decide to get a minor repair elsewhere. Consequently, there is a tradeoff in offering opinions. While dishonest opinions yield high profits on each car that you fix, the number of cars that actually come to you for repairs depends upon the opinions that the other firms offer, i.e. on the honesty/dishonesty configuration amongst firms. If you are offering opinions way out of line with the other firms, you are likely to get few customers.

Finally, to illustrate how your payoffs will be determined, say there is a searcher with a minor problem. (This customer of course will be unaware of his true problem.) As he searches, he will get opinions from the experts and eventually will stop and decide. Say he decides to get a major repair. If so, the computer will look at all of the firms who would have given this car owner a major opinion if he asked them and divide his business up equally among them. For instance, only dishonest firms and certain incompetent honest firms would offer a car owner with a minor problem a major opinion. If there are K such firms, each will get 1/K of this business and then make the profit on it described above. For instance, if you are competent and dishonest, you would be included in the pool of people who share in this profit. You would fix the car with a minor repair and earn $450 - 150 = 300$ on it. Hence, your profit from this one car is $(1/K)(450 - 150)$. The same thing is done for car owners with minor problems who get minor repairs, car owners with major problems who get major repairs and car owners with major problems who get minor repairs.

So you can see that your honesty, opinion and repair rules—combined with those of all the other firms—have a dual effect. First, they determine how many customers follow your advice and therefore bring you cars to fix. They also determine how much profit you will make on each car you fix.

After each trial, we will tell you your final payoff, the average honesty/dishonesty mix among the competent and incompetent firms, and the average payoffs of the other firms of your competency. You will then be asked to repeat the experiment. We will do this for ten trials. Your final payoff will be the sum of your ten payoffs. You will be paid as you leave.

EXPERIMENTAL DESIGN

Note from the instructions it appears that each experiment is characterized by ten parameters:

P_h = the cost of the high priced repair
P_1 = the cost of the low priced repair
C_h = the cost of the major priced repair
C_1 = the cost of the minor priced repair
ξ = fraction of car owners with major repairs
μ = degree of competency of incompetent firms
α = fraction of firms that are incompetent
N = number of firms
L = number of consumers in market
C = cost per search

Changes in these parameters determine controlled changes in the experiment to be performed. In the instruction we described above, we have P_h = 450, P_1 = 350, C_h = 250, C_1 = 150, μ = .8, C = 4, N = 3, L = 6, α = .5 (three competent firms and three incompetent), ξ = .5.

There were three competent, three incompetent firms and six consumers. Each incompetent firm had an 80 percent chance of being competent. Each consumer had a 50 percent chance of having a major or minor problem. Two other experiments were performed. In one we had four incompetent and two competent firms while in the other the price of the high priced repair was lowered from 450 to 420. Since all else is held constant, these changes constitute a controlled change from experiment 1.

The comparison between experiments 3 and 1 is equivalent to a comparison of this market after and before a laboratory price control is administered since all is kept constant except the high priced repair price. Comparison between experiments 2 and 1 is equivalent to a laboratory licensing program since in moving from experiment 2 to experiment 1 the fraction of incompetent firms is reduced (and a reduction is, we presume, the purpose of licensing or other educational programs).

Table 6–2. Experimental design

Experiment 1		Experiment 2	Experiment 3
(10 groups)		(10 groups)	(10 groups)
$P_h = 450$, $P_1 = 350$, credit $= 650$		same as base-	same as base-
$C_h = 250$, $C_1 = 150$		line except	line except
$\mu = .8$, $C = 4$		$\alpha = .66$	$P_h = 420$
$N = 3$, $\alpha = .5$, $\xi = .5$			

3 competent firms; 3 incompetent firms; information—high

RESULTS

The first question of importance that we must address when discussing these laboratory markets is how these markets performed. Clearly, if market performance is good, then governmental intervention is not needed, while if it is poor, pressures for intervention may arise from consumer groups. A first indication of market performance is the average honestly levels of incompetent and competent firms. Honesty levels for experimental runs 1, 2, and 3 are given in Tables 6–3 and 6–4. These honestly levels varied from a low of .68 for competents in experiment 3 (see Table 6–4) to a high of .79 for incompetents in experiment 1 (see Tables 6–3 and 6–4). In addition, the variances were quite small, ranging from a low of .02 to a high of .065. Hence, while these honestly levels were substantially above zero, they might not be considered sufficently high to warrant nonintervention. This fact led Pitchik and Schotter to investigate the economic performance of these markets by constructing a set of performance measures and then seeing how market performance changed as we made various types of controlled interventions. While we will not investigate these measures here, it is important to point out that, while focusing on market honesty is important, it does not tell the whole picture and their other measures were developed specifically to present a more complete picture of the welfare implications of our experiments.[15] Space does not allow us to present them here, however.

Table 6–3. Effects of licensing: comparison of the results of experiments 1 and 2

	Experiment 1	Experiment 2	Difference
Mean honesty of competent firms	.77(30**) (.04*)	.71(20**) (.05*)	.006(1.594†)
Mean honesty of incompetent firms	.79(30**) (.02*)	.71(40**) (.02*)	.08(1.693†)

* indicates variance
** indicates number of observations
† indicates Wilcoxon statistic

Table 6–4. Effects of price controls: comparisons of experiments 1 and 3

	Experiment 1	Experiment 3	Difference
Mean honesty of competent firms	.77(30**) (.04*)	.68(30**) (.05*)	.09 (1.412†)
Mean honesty of incompetent firms	.79(30**) (.02*)	.69(30**) (.02*)	.10 (1.959†)

* indicates variance
** indicates number of observations
† indicates Wilcoxon statistic

Licensing: Reductions in α (comparisons of experiments 1 and 2)

One possible intervention into this market might consist of a licensing policy whose aim is to decrease the fraction of incompetents in the market (reduce α). As we see, experiment 2 is a market which is identical to experiment 1 except for the fact that in experiment 2 two-thirds of the firms (four firms) are incompetent ($\alpha = \frac{2}{3}$) while in experiment 1 only half of the firms (three firms) are incompetent ($\alpha = \frac{1}{2}$). Hence, comparing the results of these two markets should be equivalent to comparing the effects of a licensing program which reduces the fraction of incompetents in the market.

The results of this comparison, for both competent and incompetent honesty levels and consumer protection measures, are presented in Table 6–3.

As can be seen from Table 6–3, this licensing program has an unambiguously beneficial effect. The mean honesty levels of competent and incompetent firms are increased from .71 to .77 and .79 respectively, and these differences were found to be statistically significant at the 6 percent level for competent firms and the 4 percent level for incompetent firms using a Wilcoxon–Mann–Whitney one-tailed test. Consequently, we conclude that, in the experiment, the effect of licensing has significant beneficial effects on the honesty of experts.

Price Controls: Lowering P_h (comparisons of experiments 1 and 3

Comparisons of the results of Experiments 3 and 1 portray the impact in these markets of governmental efforts to control prices. This is true since both experiments were identical except for the fact that in experiment 3, $P_h = 420$ while in experiment 1, $P_h = 450$. Hence, experiment 3 represents a market in which prices for major repairs are administratively reduced. The results of these comparisons present some paradoxical facts which are portrayed in Table 6–4.

As can be seen, a reduction in the price of the major repair had an unambiguously detrimental effect on market honesty. Honesty levels among both competent and incompetent firms drop from .77 to .68 and from .79 to .69 respectively. These differences were statistically significant at the 10 percent level of significance for competents and the 3 percent level of significance for incompetents.

These results are paradoxical because we usually expect that a reduction in a price would have beneficial effects for consumers. This way of thinking fails to take the secondary aspects of the situation into account, however. For instance, the drop in the price of a major repair implies that the cost of making the mistake of getting a major repair, when a minor repair would have been sufficient, also drops. Suppose this drop makes consumers either search less or makes them more easily convinced to get a major repair (i.e., they require fewer major opinions in order to get a major repair). We may well expect that firms would take advantage of this drop in consumer vigilance and lower their honesty levels.

Table 6–5 indicates both the average number of searches for consumers in both of these experiments and the average number of major opinions needed by searchers in order to get a major repair.

As we can see, consumers tend to search less in experiment 3 than in experiment 1 (the mean number of searches dropped from 2.11 to 1.96). This drop, while small in absolute terms, was statistically significant at the 16 percent level of significance using a one-tailed Wilcoxon–Mann–Whitney test.

Table 6–5. Consumer search and decision rules: comparisons of experiments 1 and 3

	Experiment 1	*Experiment 5*	*Difference*
Number of searches per consumer	2.11(.41*)	1.96(.34*)	.15 (1.014†)
Mean number of major opinions needed to get a major repair	2.03(.57)*	1.66(.45*)	.37 (1.456†)

* indicates variance; † indicates Wilcoxon statistic

In addition, they also tended to be more easily convinced to buy a major repair with the number of major opinions needed to get a major repair dropping from 2.03 to 1.66. This difference was also significant using the Wilcoxon–Mann–Whitney test at the 8 percent level of significance. Consequently it may be that price controls are a two-edged sword in terms of consumer welfare; while lower prices increase welfare by allowing consumers to get more goods more cheaply, higher prices may lead to more searching and more skepticism of opinions. In our comparisons of experimental runs 1 and 5 it seemed as if the second effect dominated.

MARKET NORMS

It is never easy or wise to generalize from the results of one experimental study. However, we do feel that certain conclusions can be reached on the basis of their experimental results. First it appears that in the type of experimental markets discussed here, subject-firms establish a "norm of honesty" for themselves and seem to adhere to it. This honesty norm seems to be influenced by the parameters of the market, i.e., the prices competency levels etc. To illustrate this, notice that in all experiments there is little difference between the mean honesty levels of competent and incompetent firms. The variance around these means is also small indicating that most firms chose honesty levels close to the mean. Given a set of market parameters, then, it appears that *all* firms tend to adhere to the market honesty norm. However, the norm does move as we change market parameters (compare the honesty levels of experiments 3 and 1 (Table 6–4) or of experiments 2 and 1 (Table 6–3).

Furthermore, the government does have the ability to change the level of honesty contained in the norm established by the industry. As Pitchik and Schotter have seen, in their experiment licensing programs prove to be an effective tool for government intervention (compare the results of experiments 1 and 2). In terms of honesty levels, markets function better when there are fewer incompetents. Price controls, on the other hand, seem to be more problematic. As indicated, probably owing to their adverse impact on consumer searching, reductions in the price of a major repair lead to lower market honesty. Such results should stand to warn naive government bureaucrats about the system effects of price controls in market with uncertainty, but also warn the naive free-marketeer about the blind adherence to free market prescriptions.

CONCLUSION

I hope that this chapter has accomplished two things. First, I hope that it has whetted your appetite for the type of exciting results that are being generated by scholars currently engaged in experimental economics. These few examples have merely scratched the surface of the work being done there. Secondly, I hope that the experiments discussed have provided some empirical grounds to make us stop and think before blindly adhering to market solutions for all of our social ills, and have further instilled in you a healthy skepticism about the foundations upon which the free market argument rests. Space and time have limited our discussion here, but readers are strongly urged to pursue these matters on their own.

NOTES

1. Much of the material in this chapter is taken from previous papers and articles by the author in collaboration with Clive Bull, Keith Weigelt, and Carolyn Pitchik. The material on the equity efficiency tradeoff is taken from "The Benefits of Equal Opportunity" (with Keith Weigelt), *Business and Society Review*, Spring 1988, pp. 45–48, and based on experiments performed by Clive Bull, Keith Weigelt and myself. I thank them for their collaboration.
2. See Clive Bull, Andrew Schotter, and Keith Weigelt, "Tournaments and Piece Rate: An Experimental Study," *Journal of Political Economy*, Vol. 95, February 1987b, pp. 1–33; and A. Schotter and K. Weigelt, "The Benefits of Equal Opportunity," *Business and Society Review*, Spring 1988, pp. 45–48.
3. See C. Bull, A. Schotter, and K. Weigelt, "Asymmetric Tournaments, Equal Opportunity Laws and Affirmative Action: Some Experimental Results." C. V. Starr Center for Applied Economics, Research Report 8733, 1987a.
4. C. Bull, A. Schotter, and K. Weigelt, "Asymmetric Tournaments."
5. See E. Hoffman and M. Spitzer, "The Coase Theorem: Some Experimental Tests," *Journal of Law and Economics*, vol. 25, 1982, pp. 93–98; and "Entitlements, Rights and Fairness: An Experimental Examination of Subject's Concepts of Distribution Justice," *Journal of Legal Studies*, vol. 14, November 2 1985, pp. 259–297.
6. E. Hoffman and M. Spitzer, "Entitlement, Rights and Fairness."
7. E. Hoffman and M. Spitzer, "The Coase Theorem."

8. See M. Isaac, K. McCue, and C. Plott, "Public Goods Provision in an Experimental Environment," *Journal of Public Economics*, vol. 26, 1985, pp. 51–74.
9. Lief Johansen, "The Theory of Public Goods Misplaced Emphasis," *Journal of Public Economics*, vol. 7, 1977, p. 147.
10. A. Roth, "Laboratory Experimentation in Economics: A Methodological Overview," *The Economic Journal*, vol. 98, no. 393, December 1988, pp. 994–1032; and P. Bohm, "Estimating Demand for Public Goods: An Experiment," *European Economic Review*, vol. 3, 1972, pp. 111–130.
11. F. Schneider and W. Pommerehne, "Free Riding and Collective Action: An Experiment in Public Microeconomics," *Quarterly Journal of Economics*, vol. 116, 1981, pp. 689–704.
12. See C. Pitchik and A. Schotter, "Regulating Markets with Asymmetric Information: An Experimental Study." C. V. Starr Center Research Report, 1985.
13. C. Pitchik and A. Schotter, "Regulating Markets."
14. C. Plott and L. Wilde, "Professional Diagnosis vs. Self Diagnosis: An Experimental Examination of Some Special Features of Markets with Uncertainty," *Research in Experimental Economics*, vol. 2, ed. Vernon Smith, Greenwich Connecticut, JAI Press, 1982.
15. For a full discussion, see C. Pitchik and A. Schotter, "Regulating Markets."

7

Blame-Free Justice

If we had a society of people who actually believed in the free market axioms listed in chapter 1—individualism, property rights, rationality, selfishness, economic competition, etc.—what notions of economic justice would they subscribe to? Individualists would advocate what I shall call endogenous justice theories. These are theories that use only the preferences or personal ethical codes of the individuals in the society under consideration in judging whether a given social state is fair and that require a unanimous agreement among those individuals before justifying a particular state. In short, a social outcome is fair if *all* people think it is, and no external authority has the right to make that decision for them. Justice is then a totally operational concept. No philosophers or economists need be consulted, because the opinion of such external "experts" is irrelevant.

Endogenous justice theories are to be distinguished from exogenous justice theories, which define concepts of justice by relying on principles formulated without taking into account the individual ethical preferences of the population under discussion. These theories impose those principles from above upon the population. Exogenous concepts of justice would not be accepted by a society of individualists, because they would reject the right of any external authority to impose its view of justice on their society. For instance, a socialist's egalitarian views on just income distributions are bound to be rejected by a society of nineteenth-century classical liberals, just as a priest's notions of justice might be rejected by a society of atheists. Endogenous theories of justice change with the population of people under investigation. What is just for one society is not for another. Individualists would argue that only the agents of a society have the right to define the concept of justice they use and that concept must be unanimously agreed to.

If people believe in rationality and the right of others to be selfish in the pursuit of their own self-interest, as proponents of the free market do, then outcomes that are defined by rational selfish action cannot be rejected as unfair. They may be undesirable (as the prisoner's dilemma game of chapter 4 indicates) but not unjust.

If people believe in property rights and have faith in the invisible hand (when coupled with the rationality and selfishness that support it) then it would appear that social agents have a right to whatever outcomes the free market defines for them. This fact generates the free market advocate's belief in a process-oriented view of justice as proposed by Nozick. Such theories of justice, as we discussed in chapter 1, judge all social outcomes or income distributions in terms of the process that defines them and not in terms of the properties of the actual income distributions or other outcomes that result.

For any theory of justice to be acceptable to a group of people who believe in the axioms listed in chapter 1, it must not be exogenous and outcome-oriented. As individualists they would reject the imposition of outcomes or of external standards of fairness. Only the individuals involved have the right to do that. They would also reject either an endogenous or exogenous predetermination of outcomes, because doing so (by, say, redistributing income) is bound to violate citizens' property rights. Hence, a group of individualists believing in the axioms listed in chapter 1 would only accept a theory of justice that is endogenous and process-oriented.

Few of the justice theories available today actually fit these characteristics very well. For instance, egalitarianism is obviously an outcome-oriented, exogeneous theory of justice, as are Rawlsian justice, utilitarianism, and the notions of Shapley and Nash relating to game theory.[1] Nozick's theory, on the other hand, is obviously process-oriented, but exogenous, since it starts with the presumption that a "fair" outcome is one generated by a "fair" process and then imposes this belief on the economies or societies studied.[2] Clearly, however, such a belief is not shared by all societies and hence is not endogenous.

Finally, Duncan Foley and Hal Varian espouse a notion of justice in which an allocation of goods is fair if it is "envy-free" in the sense that no individual in society envies the bundles of any other agent.[3] Here, each individual evaluates all other individuals' bundles in terms of his or her own preferences. If all individuals prefer their own bundles to those of all others, the allocation is deemed envy-free and fair. Clearly Foley's and Varian's notion is endogenous (only individual preferences are consulted and the criterion is unanimity) and outcome-oriented. All of these theories are summarized in Figure 7–1.

	process-oriented theories	*end-state-oriented theories*
exogenous theories	Nozick	egalitarianism utilitarianism, Rawlsian justice (Shapley, Nash)
endogenous theories	?	envy-freeness

Figure 7–1. Classification of theories of justice

Notice that I have not listed any theories as endogenous and process-oriented. I will now present one such theory, which I shall call blame-free justice. I demonstrate that although this theory should be acceptable to proponents of the free market it can define outcomes that any free market advocate should reject. Hence, this concept of justice demonstrates, by example, that the free market axioms may determine inconsistent results.

BLAME-FREE JUSTICE

I shall define blame-freeness as a notion of justice that looks at the process defining a particular social outcome, evaluates the behavior that each person displayed during this process, and then declares the outcome just or not depending on whether the behavior defining it was reasonable. However, since blame-freeness is an endogenous theory, when we judge any individual's behavior we must do so strictly in terms of the preferences and ethical codes of the individuals in the society we are investigating and they must all agree that their behavior was reasonable. The most straightforward way to evaluate a person's behavior is to put oneself in his position and ask if you would have acted as he did under the circumstances. If the answer is yes, then you cannot blame him for his actions and in that sense his actions are justifiable. Furthermore, if no one can blame anyone else for his actions in determining a particular social outcome, then that outcome will be called "blame-free" and is just in that sense. Blame-free outcomes can thus be defined as follows: An outcome v in society Z with institutional structure I is justifiable if no social agent in Z can blame any other agent for the actions he took in defining outcome v.

Notice that blame-freeness is an endogenous, process-oriented theory of justice. It is endogenous because the only information needed in order to judge a social outcome is the preferences of the agents in society and their unanimous consent. It is process-oriented because blame-freeness never looks at the outcome under investigation but rather only at the actions of people during the process defining this outcome. Hence on this criterion blame-freeness is more consistent with our free market axioms than are any of the other justice concepts listed. Let us investigate what blame-freeness implies by looking at two examples.

Situation 1: Assume that a terminally ill cancer patient is lying in his hospital bed riddled with pain. At night a nurse mistakenly leaves a lethal drug by his bedside, which he knowingly takes and kills himself. Is his action justifiable by a society of agents reared in the Judeo-Christian moral tradition?

Situation 2: A set of oligopolists feels that their only obligation to society is to make money. One oligopolist is offered the exclusive rights to exploit a valuable resource that all firms need in order to exist. It buys the resource, excludes all other firms from its use, and establishes itself as a monopolist. Can such an act be justified by the oligopolists under consideration?

According to blame-free justice, a person who needs to answer these questions begins by asking himself what he would have done if placed in the situation described. He must check his own personal ethical system and decide upon an action. He would then compare his action to the one chosen by the person under consideration. If the two actions are identical, then the original act is a blame-free act. If this is true for all agents in society, then the action and the resulting outcome are universally "blame-free" and justifiable according to our theory of justice.

However, notice exactly what this blame-free notion entails. First, we must locate the relevant population within which to solicit opinions. Acts that are blame-free in college dormitories may be blameworthy in banks. Blame-freeness then differs from Hare's notion of universalizability since it is a notion conditional on the population under investigation and not generalizable to all conceivable populations.

Blame-free acts and the resulting social states they define may violate external absolute ethical codes and, hence, may not be justifiable when judged by them. For instance, in situation 1, suicide violates Judeo-Christian beliefs. According to those beliefs suicide is not justifiable whether or not each member of a certain population would have killed himself if he were a terminal cancer patient. Blame-freeness, then, is a totally endogenous ethic. Acts are justifiable in a society if all people in that society think they are, because only their opinions are relevant.

Along these lines, notice that because blame-freeness looks only at the individual ethics of the agents in society for its justification, these societies are likely to fall victim to their own personal ethical standards. For instance, if, as in situation 2, society consisted of a group of selfish, profit-maximizing oligopolists, the monopoly created there would have to be justifiable despite our intuitive feeling (summarized by the Sherman Anti-Trust Act) that the act is unfair. Societies that make nasty personal ethical beds for themselves are forced to lie in them if blame-freeness is to be used as a moral criterion.

Actions that are blame-free may define social states that are not Pareto superior to the state existing before the act was taken. Clearly, in the oligopoly case, each firm is made worse off by a monopolist's actions, and society as a whole suffers as well if consumer surplus is to be used as a criterion. Yet, with respect to the oligopolists, no firm blames the monopolist for his action. They would have done the same thing if they had been in his place.

Blame-freeness has a unanimity requirement. *All* people in a relevant population must not blame a person before his action can be called blame-free. This is clearly a strong requirement that allows prudes to have a moral veto over all actions. The requirements can be weakened by using a representative or average person (the legal "reasonable man") performing the blame-free experiment, but that will not be necessary for our purposes here.

In our definition of blame-freeness, we required that the institutional structure (I) of the economy under consideration must be considered before one is asked to judge the blame-freeness of any agent's act. This was done because the social states that we are asked to judge do not exist in a vacuum. Rather they are the outcome of a multitude of social and economic institutions that define rules constraining our behavior and awarding us payoffs for our actions. In judging these outcomes, in essence we are being asked to judge the fairness of the institutions used to define them.

Blame-freeness is then a heavily institutional notion in that each agent's actions are judged in an institutional context and the blame-freeness of particular acts changes as this context changes. In this sense, it is similar to Rawls's notion of maxi-min justice, except for the fact that Rawls worked toward designing fair institutions, while we are concerned here with examining the fairness of the outcomes produced by pre-existing institutions.

One should not conclude that our notion of blame-freeness is a justification of lawlessness. If a person violates the law in a blame-free way, it does not follow that he should not be punished. The law is still the law and obeying it may have a rule-utilitarian justification that dominates the blame-freeness of that particular act. However, if a law or institution repeatedly leads people to violate it in a blame-free way, then a good case can be made for a change in this law or institution. This is the conclusion we will pursue later when we talk about the blame-freeness of income distributions.

BLAME-FREENESS AND RATIONALITY

Clearly there is a close relationship between blame-freeness and the rationality assumption made in the free market argument. In fact, when one person assumes another's position, he in essence says, "If I were in his place but still had my tastes and preferences, and *if I were to choose the action that maximized my satisfaction (my selfish utility function) or was best for me,* would I do what he did?" Hence, if one views the rationality assumption as the assumption that people maximize, then the blame-free experiment that people are asked to perform is a natural one for a set of free market advocates to perform in judging the reasonableness of people's actions and hence should be acceptable to them.

BLAME-FREENESS, INCOME DISTRIBUTIONS, AND PROPERTY RIGHTS

Although blame-freeness is a notion consistent with the axioms listed in chapter 1 and hence one that no free market advocate should have any theoretical objection to (although that does not mean he must like it), it can be used to justify social outcomes that involve violations of property rights. Hence, moral systems or theories of justice that satisfy the free market axioms listed in chapter 1 may fail to be consistent. Let us see how this can be.

Assume that we have three people living in an economy. Person 1 has great musical skills, person 2 great athletic skills, and person 3 great oratorical skills. Assume that society's tastes and demands are such that people with athletic and oratorical skills are highly prized, but those with musical skills are not. In the open labor market for these skills the athlete earns $100,000 a year, the orator-politician earns $70,000, and the musician earns $0. A corner solution exists for the musician. This unequal distribution of income is not unfair according to Nozick because it was arrived at totally voluntarily. The musician does not feel like sitting passively and starving to death, but decides to rob both the athlete and the orator, making the final distribution $90,000 for the athlete, $65,000 for the orator, and $15,000 for himself. Is this allocation fair? According to Nozick, the answer is obviously no. The final distribution of income was arrived at by non-voluntary means and hence is not justifiable. But can anyone really blame the musician? To put it another way, if fate had worked out differently and the athlete or orator had been allocated a zero wage, might they not do exactly the same thing? If so, then he cannot be blamed for his actions by any member of society, and the resulting distribution of income is blame-free.

Notice that the justification of the musician's action is that he is just responding rationally to the relative wages and prices that he faces. Hence if we are rational, we cannot logically blame him for his actions, assuming that our best response to a zero wage would also be to engage in theft rather than to starve.

In the same vein, it is interesting to look at how John Rawls might view this argument. Assume that our three people meet with each other before any information is known about whose talents will be demanded by society (i.e., before what Rawls calls the "veil of ignorance" is lifted). When they meet they discuss the fact that if they let the market determine their wage rates and hence their incomes, one will receive an income of $100,000, one an income of $70,000, and one an income of $0. If the market determined their income, the total GNP of the society would be $170,000, which is the largest possible GNP. Assume that these agents know that the one who receives the zero income is not going to sit idly by and accept it. In fact, they know he will rob the others.

Rawls's argument would be that the rules that society used to generate these incomes should be changed to increase the welfare of the worst-off member of society (i.e., the one who is the corner dweller). In doing this, however, the total GNP of the economy would have to fall, since we know that the set of rules defined by the market maximized GNP. Hence, in the Rawlsian view, all people work but the market is interfered with to such an extent that the GNP produced decreases. The economic pie to be distributed as a result of the contract or set of rules agreed to by Rawls's agents under the veil of ignorance will be smaller, but this inefficiency is accepted because it increases the income of the least-well-off member of society.

The argument for income transfers is simple. The free market, by determining an unequal distribution of income (and possibly a corner solution) leads some fraction of the population to engage in crime as a rational response to their plight. If the activities they engage in are blame-free in the sense that all other agents in society would have done the same if they had been reduced to their circumstances, then the market has created a situation where blame-free thefts exist. The population is then faced with a dilemma. Should they spend real resources trying to beef up their police forces, build new jails, and hire more judges to prevent crimes that any of them would have committed if they had been the criminals? Or should they simply transfer to each person a blame-free income and spend resources to incarcerate only those remaining individuals who commit blameworthy thefts? In other words, each individual feels he has a right to his blame-free income because no social institution (i.e., the market or the state) has the right to force a free agent to become a criminal as the rational, maximizing response to the incentive structure of the institution. By forcing the individual into a life of blame-free crime, the institution loses its right to judge his actions.

As a result, we can see that free markets are capable of determining outcomes in which people have incentives to violate the property rights of others in a blame-free way. Hence, a set of rational economic agents who believe in the market and in the endogenous, process-oriented theories of justice supporting it may very well be able to justify social outcomes that violate people's property rights. A rationality-based justice theory may not respect people's rights to keep what the market gives them.

CONCLUSION

If free market advocates are going to subscribe to the set of axioms described in chapter 1, then they may have to suffer the consequences of these beliefs and accept those actions of individual maximizing agents that they consider to be blame-free. The American economy, with its emphasis on rationality, selfishness, profit maximizing, and individual freedom, must suffer the consequences of these beliefs and it will have very little to complain about if some of these bad consequences result from acts that all people, if they are consistent advocates of free markets, would have to consider blame-free. We are all victims of the assumptions that underlie our moral lives, and if we are willing to accept the benefits of those axioms (freedom and efficiency), we must also understand their shortcomings (poverty and crime).

NOTES

1. Lloyd Shapley, "A Value for n-Person Games," *Contributions to the Theory of Games II, Annals of Mathematics Studies*, 28, Princeton, NJ: Princeton University Press, 1953; John Nash, "The Bargaining Problem," *Econometrica*, 18, 1950, pp. 155–162.
2. Robert Nozick, "Summary of Readers' Responses," *Scientific American*, March 1974.
3. Duncan Foley, "Resource Allocation and the Public Sector," *Yale Economic Essays*, Spring 1967; Hal Varian, "Equity, Envy and Efficiency," *Journal of Economic Theory*, 9, 1974, pp. 1–23.
4. R. M. Hare, *Freedom and Reason*, Oxford: Oxford University Press, 1963.

8

Rational Expectations and Newcomb's Problem

One article of faith of the free market argument is that the economy is basically self-correcting—that it can cure inflation and recession if left alone. The mechanism that does this, of course, is individual rationality. Consider Figure 8–1. Let us assume that the economy is at a full employment equilibrium with price level P_E and real GNP Q_E, which we will assume is the natural rate of output. There is a sudden demand shock to the economy and the demand curve shifts to the right. If the supply curve remains unchanged, the new equilibrium will be at $Q'_E P'_E$. However, this new equilibrium involves a higher price level than Q_E—inflation has set in. As rational workers learn this, they will realize that their real wages have fallen and demand higher wages. This will increase the cost of production and shift the supply curve back to S'. The economy will return to the natural rate of output, but at a higher price level.

Similarly, Figure 8–2 assumes that there is a sudden fall in aggregate demand, which shifts D to the left. Real GNP then falls, as does the price level until a new equilibrium is reached at Q''_E. At this equilibrium, however, unemployment rises above the natural rate, and as a result money wages fall as workers compete for the now scarce jobs. However, as wages

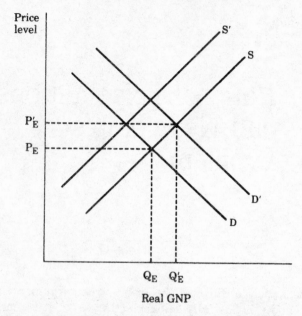

Figure 8–1. Inflation caused by increased demand

fall, the cost of doing business decreases and the aggregate supply curve shifts to the right until equilibrium is restored at the natural rate. As we can see, the ultimate equilibrium is always at the natural rate. The profit- and utility-maximizing motives of firms and workers ensure this.

RATIONAL EXPECTATIONS

Recently the role of rationality in economics has been elevated to a new level—put on a pedestal, in fact—by a school of economists known as the rational expectationists. Rational expectations are the expectations that an economic agent would have if he had a *complete* and *correct* model of the economy within which he was functioning and used all information available to him in conjunction with this model to predict what would happen in the economy. Let us say there

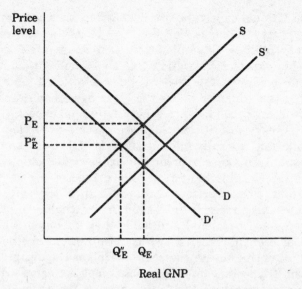

Figure 8–2. Deflation caused by decreased demand

is a farmer in a country where the weather is always the same—45 days of sun followed by 10 days of rain. If the farmer has a good memory and can recognize this pattern by counting rainy and sunny days, he could predict perfectly whether there would be rain or sun on any given day. Hence, after the tenth rainy day in a row, he would expect sun on the next day, which is clearly the only rational expectation to hold. People need not hold such rational expectations, however, possibly because they cannot recognize the pattern of rain (they have no memory or are too lazy to do the appropriate calculations). Hence, they might simply assume that on any given day the weather on the next day will be the same as it is today. Such expectations are not rational, since they are not the expectations that people would make if they had recognized the weather pattern, but they do predict fairly well, being in fact wrong only 2 out of 55 days. In more complex environments, however, "irrational" expectations are certainly capable of predicting badly.

The rational expectations school (led by such economists as Robert Lucas, Thomas Sargent, and Neil Wallace) contend that it is realistic to assume that each agent in an economy forms his expectations rationally. This implies that he is a well-informed economic theorist endowed with the same "true" model of the economy as are the other agents and capable of manipulating that model to generate rational expectations. It would be easy to criticize this assumption, since clearly not everyone can be a fully informed economic theorist, and many of us simply make our prediction using some adaptive rule (e.g., interest rates tomorrow will be the same as they are today plus some fraction of the difference between what I thought today's rates would be and their actual level). Even if all agents were rational and made their predictions using a model of economic reality, we could question whether they would all decide to use the same model, as the disagreement between Keynesians and monetarists makes clear. Further, it may not even make sense to talk about a "true model," since the economic reality we face may simply be a function of the economic models that people use in predicting reality (the world may be only subjectively, not objectively, knowable). These criticisms are not the ones I wish to pursue here, however, since I am searching for immanent criticisms of the free market argument and not criticisms that merely challenge its assumptions. Hence, let us see how rational expectations may be self-defeating or even contradictory. To do this, let us first look at the rational expectations model of economic activity and some difficulties with it.

POLICY NEUTRALITY AND RATIONAL EXPECTATIONS

The rational-expectations school relies on the individual's rationality and the economy's self-correcting capabilities to justify its laissez-faire macroeconomic policy prescriptions in the following way. Consider an economy depicted by the aggregate supply and demand curves depicted in Figure 8–3. Assume that the economy is at an initial equilibrium, with price

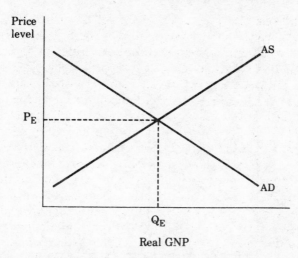

Figure 8–3. Aggregate supply and demand curves

P_E and quantity Q_E, and that the government increases the money supply. If workers are rational and use the classical quantity theory of exchange as their model for the price-level determination, then they will know that all prices will rise in proportion to the increase in the money supply.[1] Firms, on the other hand, will expect that workers, knowing prices will increase, will demand higher wages. Firms will also expect that lenders, knowing prices will rise, will ask for higher nominal interest rates. Hence, if the monetary policy is anticipated and if all agents (workers and firms) form their expectations of prices and wages rationally, we can expect both the aggregate demand and supply curves to shift as depicted in Figure 8–4 and a new equilibrium to be established at the same level of GNP as before Q_E but at a higher price level (P_E') and higher interest rates.

Consequently, anticipated monetary policy and fiscal policy are ineffective even in the short run in changing the real level of GNP in the economy. Monetary or fiscal policy, if anticipated, does not change the level of real GNP in the economy.[2] Furthermore, banks, other corporations, and

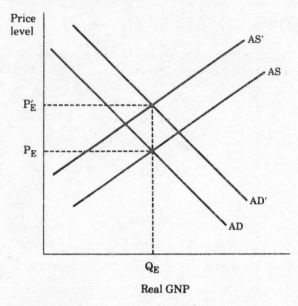

Figure 8–4. Shift in demand and supply curves from anticipation of monetary policy

unions, using rational expectations, make it their business to anticipate what the government will do. Unless the government continually surprises the public or acts randomly, it cannot expect to have any impact on the economy. Not only can the economy correct itself, but the government cannot do anything to correct the economy, even if it wants to.

I want to address not this policy-neutrality question but whether the type of rational expectations posited above is logically possible in a world in which the government assumes that the public holds rational expectations. If it is not, then this fact may have implications for the type of arguments made above. To pose this question properly, I will first describe a philosophical problem called Newcomb's problem and then demonstrate how it is related to the problem of the logical existence of rational expectations.[3]

NEWCOMB'S PROBLEM

Consider the following decision problem first described by William A. Newcomb and discussed by Gardner.[4] Two closed boxes, B1 and B2, are on a table. B1 contains $1,000. B2 contains either $1,000,000 or nothing. The decision maker does not know the contents of B2. The decision maker has an irrevocable choice between two actions:

1. Take the content of B2.
2. Take the contents of both boxes.

Assume that a superior Being whom the decision maker knows to have "extremely good predictive powers" has made a prediction about what the decision maker will decide. If the Being expects the decision maker to choose both boxes, the Being leaves B2 empty. If He expects the decision maker to take only B2, He puts $1,000,000 in it. (If He expects the decision maker to randomize his choice by, say, flipping a coin, the Being also leaves B2 empty.) In all cases, B1 contains $1,000. The decision maker understands the situation fully, the Being knows he understands, the decision maker knows that He knows, and so on. (In all that we say, we assume that utility is linear in money; thus the numbers below are utilities).

Which choice should the decision maker make? The conundrum is that there is a strong argument for either decision, yet they cannot both be correct. The decision problem is illustrated in Figure 8–5. If the decision maker takes B2 alone and that was predicted by the Being, then his payoff is $1,000,000 (the Being having put that amount in B2). On the other hand, if the decision maker takes B2 alone but the Being predicted he would take both boxes, then the Being would leave B2 empty; thus the payoff would be $0. Likewise, if the decision maker chooses both boxes and the Being predicted that he would choose only B2, the payoff would be $1,001,000 ($1,000 is always in B1 and the Being would have placed $1,000,000 in B2 in this case). Finally, if the decision

BEING

	Move 1 (Predicts you take only B2)	Move 2 (Predicts you take B1 and B2)
Move 1 (Takes only B2)	$1,000,000	$0
Move 2 (Takes B1 and B2)	$1,001,000	$1,000

DECISION MAKER

Figure 8–5. Newcomb's problem

maker chooses both boxes and the Being predicted it, the pay-off would only be $1,000 (B2 being left empty).

Consider the decision maker's dilemma. If he feels that trying to outguess the Being is useless, because the Being is practically omniscient, he must choose B2 only. As an illustration, assume that the Being anticipates correctly nine out of ten times. The expected utility (EU) from choosing B2 would be:

$$EU(B2 \text{ only}) = .9(1,000,000) + .1(0) = 900,000$$

while the expected utility of choosing both boxes is:

$$EU(B1 \& B2) = .1(1,001,000) + .9(1,000) = 101,000$$

Consequently, in terms of the expected utility hypothesis, the decision to take B2 is clearly preferable. However, we can view the problem differently.

If the Being has already predicted what the decision maker will do, then either he has placed $1,000,000 in B2 or he has not. In this case, it makes sense to choose both boxes for the following reasons: either the Being predicted the decision maker would take B2, in which case He put $1,000,000 in B2, or He predicted the decision maker would take both boxes. In the first case, the payoff is $1,001,000; in the second case, the payoff is $1,000. But in either case, the decision to take both boxes dominates the decision to take only B2. This can be seen by the fact that each element in row 2 is greater than the corresponding element in row 1, so that no matter what the Being predicts, it is better to choose row 2. Consequently, from the perspective of the dominance principle, the decision to take both boxes is superior to that of taking only B2.

At this point the reader might question how sensitive the problem is to the actual indices used in the matrix and the predictive powers of the Being. Surprisingly, the problem or decision dilemma exists for a variety of worlds. For instance, if we let $U(x_1)$, $U(x_2)$, $U(x_3)$, and $U(x_4)$ be the Von Neumann–Morgenstern utility indices for the best, second best, third best, and least attractive outcomes, and if we let α be the probability that the Being guesses correctly, then simple algebra[5] indicates that the dilemma holds as long as $\frac{\alpha}{1-\alpha} > \frac{U(x_1) - U(x_4)}{U(x_2) - U(x_3)}$. Consequently, if $U(x_1) = 40$, $U(x_2) = 30$, $U(x_3) = 20$, and $U(x_4) = 10$, then the problem will exist as long as the decision maker thinks that the Being has even as little as a 75 percent chance of being correct. Hence, the superiority of the Being may be quite limited, while the decision maker still falls victim to Newcomb's problem.

The consquence of these considerations is that in Newcomb's problem or in similar situations, there is a conflict between the expected utility hypothesis and the dominance principle. While either decision can be justified, no rational action exists, because no matter which choice is made there is a strong argument for making the other. Rational expectations may be "the same as the predictions of the relevant economic theory," but here there is a theory conflict with no unambiguous method for deciding between theories.[6] One choice that maximizes the decision-maker's expected utility is dominated by another that does not.

If the monetary authority believes that the public has good predictive powers, meaning a sufficiently high probability of guessing its actions [i.e., if $\frac{\alpha}{1-\alpha} > \frac{U(x_1) - U(x_4)}{U(x_2) - U(x_3)}$], then the authority becomes a decision maker caught in a situation similar to that of Newcomb's problem. Consequently, it has no rational course of action or policy prescription. We shall now investigate the consequences of this dilemma for the existence and consistency of rational expectations of government's action.

NEWCOMB'S PROBLEM AND MONETARY POLICY

Consider a monetary authority that wishes to influence the level of two economic variables—the inflation rate $\dot{P}$ and the unemployment rate U—through adjusting the rate of growth of the money supply. This monetary authority faces a monolithic public with one mind. The impact that monetary policy has on the existing inflation-unemployment configuration will depend upon whether the authority's actions are correctly anticipated by the public. Obviously, by analogy to Newcomb's problem, we are depicting the monetary authority here as the decision maker. The public corresponds to the Being, whose ability to predict the monetary authority's action is summarized by the probability with which the monetary authority thinks that the public will correctly anticipate its policy choice.

The monetary authority has two possible actions: to increase the rate of growth of the money supply (M_H) or to decrease the rate of growth of the money supply (M_L). We want to describe what effects these monetary policies will have on the existing inflation-unemployment configuration as a consequence of public anticipations.

Consider the following simple macro model made by Robert Lucas and widely used in the literature on rational expectations.[7]

$$y_t^s = y_t^* + \alpha(P_t - P_t^e); \alpha > 0 \tag{1}$$

$$y_t^d = m_t - P_t + V_t \tag{2}$$

$$y_t^s = y_t^d \tag{3}$$

where y_t^s, y_t^d are the natural logarithms (logs) of aggregate supply and demand, y_t^* = log of "full-employment" or "natural" level of output, P_t = log of the price level, P_t^e = log of the price level *expected by the public*, m_t = log of the money stock, V_t = constant—log of velocity. Roughly this model has the following interpretation. Equation (1) is what is known as the Lucas supply function. It states that the amount of goods supplied by producers in the economy in period t will deviate from the economy's "natural" or "normal" amount only if producers do not anticipate prices correctly (i.e., if P_t^e [expected prices in period t] differ from P_t [realized prices in period t]). Equation (2) is a demand function for the goods produced in the economy (the classical quantity equation) and states that given the velocity of exchange and the money supply, the demand for goods is inversely related to the price level. Finally, equation (3) is an equilibrium relationship and states that if we are to be in equilibrium in the economy in period t, the supply of goods y_t^s must be equal to the demand y_t^d. For simplicity we will let $V_t = 0$.

Assuming that P_t is the value that equates y_t^s in (1) to y_t^d in (2), we obtain:

$$P_t = \frac{1}{1+\alpha}m_t + \frac{\alpha}{1+\alpha}P_t^e - \frac{1}{1+\alpha}y_t^* \tag{4}$$

It is usually assumed that the public knows the coefficients of the model and therefore, in forming a rational expectation of P_t, it uses equation (4):

$$P_t^e = \frac{1}{1+\alpha}m_t^e + \frac{\alpha}{1+\alpha}P_t^e - \frac{1}{1+\alpha}y_t^* \tag{5}$$

Solving (5) for P_t^e yields:

$$P_t^e = m_t^e - y_t^* \tag{6}$$

Table 8–1. Consequences of correctly and incorrectly anticipated monetary policy

Policy Expected by the Public	Actual Policy	Description of Outcomes
M_L	M_H	$p_t > p_t^e, U_t < U_t^*, p_t - p_{t-1}^* > \dot{p}^*$ (x_1)
M_L	M_L	$p_t = p_t^e, U_t = U_t^*, p_t - p_{t-1}^* < \dot{p}^*$ (x_2)
M_H	M_H	$p_t = p_t^e, U_t = U_t^*, p_t - p_{t-1}^* > \dot{p}^*$ (x_3)
M_H	M_L	$p_t < p_t^e, U_t > U_t^*, p_t - p_{t-1}^* < \dot{p}^*$ (x_4)

Equation (6) makes it clear that the expectation of m_t^e is crucial to the formation of rational expectation of P_t. Hence forming rational expectations in this model includes forming a rational expectation of the monetary authority's policy action. Using (5) in (4):

$$P_t = \frac{1}{1+\alpha}m_t + \frac{\alpha}{1+\alpha}m_t^e - y_t^* \tag{7}$$

Finally, using (6) and (7) in (1) yields:

$$y_t = y_t^* + \frac{1}{1+\alpha}(m_t - m_t^e) \tag{8}$$

We assume that the deviations $y_t - y_t^e$ are related to unemployment by a constant of proportionality (this is Okun's Law)[8]:

$$y_t - y_t^* = \kappa(U_t^* - U_t) \tag{9}$$

where κ is greater than 0 and is a constant. Equation (9) assumes that when $y_t = y_t^*$, unemployment is equal to natural rate U_t^*. Using (9), we can rewrite (8) as:

$$U_t = U_t^* + \beta(m_t^e - m_t), \text{ where } \beta = \frac{1}{\kappa}(1 + \alpha), \text{ or} \tag{10}$$

$$U_t = U_t^* + \beta[(m_t^e - m_{t-1}) - (m_t - m_{t-1})]$$

We can now use this model to analyze how an existing inflation-unemployment configuration will change when the government embarks on one of its two available monetary

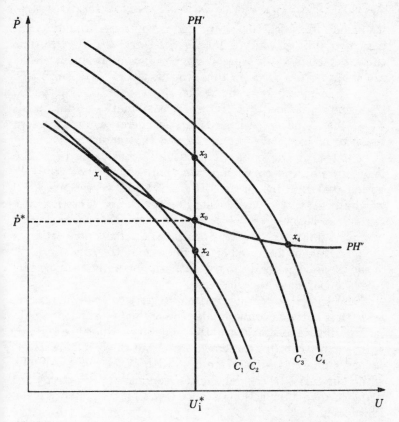

Figure 8–6. Correctly anticipated and misperceived Phillips curves

policies. We examine the effects of each policy for the case when it is correctly or incorrectly anticipated by the public. To do this, we assume that at time $(t - 1)$, the system is at the natural rate of unemployment U_t^* and the steady-state inflation rate at that unemployment level is $\dot{P}^*$ with initial price level P_{t-1}^*. Using equations (10), (2), (6), and (7), we can construct Table 8–1 to illustrate the consequences of the government's monetary action as a function of its being correctly or incorrectly anticipated by the public.

These outcomes can be depicted in Figure 8–6. In this

figure we depict the decision problem of the monetary authority as one in which the status quo is point x_0, through which pass two Phillips curves labeled PH' and PH''. (A Phillips curve depicts a set of unemployment and inflation rates that are supposed to represent the tradeoffs facing the government when it decides upon policy.) The vertical Phillips curve PH' represents the locus of $(\dot{P}^* - U)$ combinations that result when the monetary authority either increases or decreases the rate of monetary expansion and that action is correctly anticipated by the public. It is usually considered to be the long-run Phillips curve, but we shall call it the "correctly anticipated Phillips curve." The curve PH'' represents what we shall call the "misperceived Phillips curve," since it represents that locus of $(\dot{P}^* - U)$ combinations that would result when the public *incorrectly anticipates* the monetary action of the government and predicts an increase in the rate of growth of the money supply when the authority actually decreases its rate of expansion, and vice versa.

Note that the PH'' curve is not a short-run Phillips curve, since that curve is drawn under the assumption that the public has static expectations of the monetary authority's actions. A true short-run Phillips curve traces out the results of *unanticipated* changes in the rate of growth of the money supply, while our curve traces out the consequences of *incorrectly anticipated* monetary actions. Hence we call it the "misperceived Phillips curve."

The preferences of the monetary authority are given by the concave (to the origin) curves C_1, C_2, C_3, and C_4, where curves closer to the origin represent higher levels of utility. Points x_1, x_2, x_3, and x_4 are the points described in Table 7–1 and depict the consequences of correctly and incorrectly anticipated monetary policy.

Given the preferences of the monetary authority depicted in the diagram it is clear that:

$$U(x_1) > U(x_2) > U(x_3) > U(x_4).$$

where $U(x_i)$ is the Von Neumann-Morgenstern utility associated with the outcome x_i, $i = 1,2,3,4$.

		PUBLIC	
		Anticipate M_L	*Anticipate M_H*
MONETARY AUTHORITY	*Choose M_L*	$U(x_2)$	$U(x_4)$
	Choose M_H	$U(x_1)$	$U(x_3)$

Figure 8–6. Newcomb's problem and the monetary authority

Our analysis can now be represented by Figure 8–6, in which the payoffs in each cell are the payoffs to the monetary authority.

At this point Newcomb's problem appears. If the monetary authority feels that the public is a sufficiently good predictor of its actions [i.e., if it thinks that $\frac{\alpha}{1-\alpha} > \frac{U(x_1) - U(x_4)}{U(x_2) - U(x_3)}$], then by the expected-utility theory it should clearly choose to decrease the rate of growth of the money supply (action M_L), since the expected return it can expect from this action is greater than what it can expect to get from action M_H. However, M_H dominates M_L. Consequently, the same theory conflict exists here as exists in Newcomb's problem, and no rational course of action exists for the monetary authority. Hence, no rational prediction of its policy action exists.

For the public to form rational price expectations, it must form rational expectations about monetary policy (see equation 6). Hence, in this standard rational-expectations model, the public's inability to form rational expectations of monetary policy makes it unable to form rational expectations about any other relevant variable model.

CONCLUSIONS

The argument presented in this chapter can be summarized by the following proposition and its corollary.

Proposition: In the model presented above, if the government has a finite number of monetary actions that it can take (M_L and M_H) and if the utility consequences of its actions can be depicted by Figures 8-6 and 8-7, then if the monetary authority believes that the public can predict its behavior with "good predictive power" [i.e., if $\frac{\alpha}{1-\alpha} > \frac{U(x_1) - U(x_4)}{U(x_2) - U(x_3)}$], no rational expectation of the government action can be formed.

Proof: If $\frac{\alpha}{1-\alpha} > \frac{U(x_1) - U(x_4)}{U(x_2) - U(x_3)}$, then $\alpha U(x_2) + (1 - \alpha) U(x_4) > \alpha U(x_3) + (1 - \alpha) U(x_1)$, and the expected utility of M_L is greater than the expected utility of M_H. But M_H dominates M_L by construction. Hence by Newcomb's problem no best theory of behavior exists for monetary authority. Since by definition rational expectations are expectations based on *the* relevant theory of the phenomena, if no such theory exists, rational expectations cannot be formed. Q.E.D.

Corollary: In the model discussed above, rational expectations of government policy are inconsistent.

Proof: Rational expectations of government policy by the public imply, by definition, that $\frac{\alpha}{1-\alpha} > \frac{U(x_1) - U(x_4)}{U(x_2) - U(x_3)}$. But $\frac{\alpha}{1-\alpha} > \frac{U(x_1) - U(x_4)}{U(x_2) - U(x_3)}$ implies "good predictive powers" on the part of the public. Because of the Proposition, these powers imply that no rational expectation can be formed. Q.E.D.

The reason for the existence of this problem in our model is a common problem involved in forming rational expectations models in which one or more of the endogenous variables are exclusively controlled by a limited number of decision makers. In such situations, a rational expectation about the level of such a variable becomes a prediction of the behavior of the decision maker who controls its value. The problem is that if the decision maker's payoffs depend upon whether his behavior is anticipated or not, then the decision maker will be forced to enter into a series of higher-order expectations in his effort to try to second-guess those agents who are forming rational expectations concerning his behavior. The knowledge that others are trying to predict a decision maker's behavior in a systematic (i.e., rational) way may force the decision maker to behave non-systematically and hence eliminate any hope of forming a rational expectation about his behavior. Again it is rationality that defeats itself.

NOTES

1. The quantity theory of exchange, $MV = PY$, simply says that if one assumes that velocity V is relatively constant, and that Y, the real GNP of the economy, is at the natural rate of output, then any increase in the money stock M will simply result in an increase in the price level P.

2. Thomas J. Sargent and Neil Wallace, *Rational Expectations and the Theory of Economic Policy: Studies in Monetary Economics,* Minneapolis: Federal Reserve Bank of Minneapolis Research Department, 1975.

3. The discussion in the remainder of this chapter will rely heavily on Roman Frydman, Gerald O'Driscoll, and Andrew Schotter, "Rational Expectations of Government Policy: An Application of Newcomb's Problem."

4. Martin Gardner, "Mathematical Games," *Scientific American,* July 1973, pp. 104–108. Also see the March, 1974, edition of *Scientific American,* in which philosopher Robert Nozick summarized reader's responses to the discussion of the problem in the July 1973 issue.

5. Expected utility of choosing only $B2 = \alpha U(x_2) + (1 - \alpha) U(x_4)$
   Expected utility of choosing both $= (1 - \alpha) U(x_1) + \alpha U(x_3)$
   Therefore, the expected utility of choosing $B2$ only is greater than the expected utility of choosing both boxes if

   $$\alpha U(x_2) + (1 - \alpha) U(x_4) > (1 - \alpha) U(x_1) + \alpha U(x_3), \text{ or}$$
   $$\frac{\alpha}{1-\alpha} > \frac{U(x_1) - U(x_4)}{U(x_2) - U(x_3)}$$

6. John F. Muth, "Rational Expectations and the Theory of Price Movement," *Econometrica,* July 1961, pp. 315.

7. Robert E. Lucas, Jr., "Some International Evidence on Output-Inflation Tradeoffs," *American Economic Review,* June 1973, pp. 326–334. We use this particular model because it is widely used in the rational-expectations literature. In models of this class, expectations of monetary policy are often assumed to be rational.

8. Empirically Okun's Law states that the percentage-point change in the unemployment rate tends to be about one-half of the percentage drop in the ratio of the actual to the natural real output rate.

9

Why Is the American Free Market System So Stable?

Whatever one's feelings are about the merits of the American free market system, it has certainly proved to be a remarkably stable system that has remained relatively immune to major alterations in the hundreds of years it has been in existence. This is not to say that the type of capitalism, the size distribution of firms, or the role of government we have today are the same as in earlier centuries. Rather, the average American's trust in the free market has remained relatively unshaken over the years despite repeated economic crises and occasional flirtations with socialism. This is true because the free market system satisfies what I feel are four basic criteria of any successful and stable economic system. In this chapter I will discuss these criteria and investigate the extent to which the American free market system satisfies them.

The first requirement is that the incentives existing in the system be consistent with one's view of the human nature of the social agents functioning in the economy. In other words, the system should not rely on agents behaving in ways or responding to incentives that are unnatural for them. The second requirement is that the system conform to the cultural history of the society it is being imposed on. For instance, trying to convince an individualistic New Hampshire Yankee to be a European-style socialist may be difficult. If he is to be convinced that he should support the implementation of a new economic system, that system will have to be based upon a set of cultural and social beliefs that he feels are natural for him. Third, the economic system must lead to results that agents feel are fair, since these results will have to be justified by those who do relatively well under the system to those who do relatively poorly. Without such a justification social unrest is bound to exist. Finally, the system should be efficient to be considered truly successful. In fact, from an economic point of view a system's only requirement is to be efficient—questions of fairness make no sense. We will discuss requirements 1–3, however, because these requirements are prerequisites for productive, viable, and stable economic systems and must be imposed on any contemplated economic system.

HUMAN NATURE AND SOCIOECONOMIC SYSTEMS

Economic systems are social organizations held together by the behavioral or psychological functioning of the agents in them. They are social-behavioral organizations. Consequently, if people are to participate in them in an orderly fashion and accept their outcomes, these systems have to include certain basic psychological characteristics in their incentive system in order to succeed. For instance, say we wanted to design an economic system whose rules we would prescribe and then let the agents in society function under them. These rules would specify allowable and unallowable actions and the rewards or payoffs that would result from the myriad of actions that agents can take. For instance, the free market can be looked upon as a set of rules, one of which states that the act of stealing someone else's goods is illegal and is liable for punishment. The rules also specify that all buyers and sellers are free to make buy and sell offers to whomever they want at whatever price they want but are not allowed to collude in setting those prices, which violates the antitrust laws. These rules set up an incentive system that rewards people for certain types of actions and punishes them for others. In order to predict what the outcome of the free market set of rules will be, we must predict how people will behave when faced with the incentives implied by the rules. But to predict this behavior we must assess human nature itself, since it is the ultimate cause of human behavior.

For instance, if people are inherently selfish and dishonest, the rules set up by the free market will determine one set of outcomes; if people are inherently altruistic and empathetic, these rules will define a different set of outcomes. The equilibrium of the economy is dramatically affected by the type of social agents functioning under the rules of the system. Consider a two-person society composed of a father who has an apple and a son who has an orange. The father likes oranges more than apples and the son likes apples more than oranges. The rules of the economy dictate that trade takes place as follows: At 12:00 noon both the father and the son go to Grand Central Station and place either their apple or orange or nothing in a luggage locker, lock it up, and then exchange keys with one another. Hence, if they both put their fruit in the locker, then when they trade keys each will have exchanged his fruit. However, one could double-cross the other and put nothing in the locker, in which case, if the other played honestly, he would get away with both pieces of fruit. If they both put nothing in the locker, they would both keep their original piece of fruit. This simple exchange economy can be depicted by Figure 9–1.

What equilibrium outcome will result from this set of rules? To answer this question, we must first specify what types of people these fathers and sons are. Let us assume that despite their blood bond, fathers and sons in the society are really extremely selfish. Under this assumption, each would prefer the outcome in which he got both pieces of fruit and the other got none. Hence, if we let 4 equal the satisfaction that

SON

	put orange in locker	put nothing in locker
put apple in locker	exchange apple for orange	son gets both apple and orange
put nothing in locker	father gets both apple and orange	both keep original fruit

FATHER

Figure 9–1. Outcomes of fruit-exchange problem

the father or son gets from their best outcome, 3 equal the satisfaction they get from their second best outcome, etc., Figure 9–2 would summarize utilities from all possible decisions. The first number in each cell of the matrix is the payoff to the father and the second number is the payoff to the son. Looking at these payoffs we see that with this view of human nature both the father and the son would put no fruit in the locker, so that an equilibrium would result in which both merely consumed their original fruit (the outcome (2,2) underlined in the matrix). This is true because no matter what the other does, it is always better not to put one's own fruit in the locker (the game is in fact a prisoner's dilemma game). But as we know from chapter 4, the outcome is not optimal, since both the father and son would have been better off if they had exchanged their fruit. Hence, given this view of human nature, the rules defined lead our selfish father and son to mutually disadvantageous outcomes.

The same set of rules, however, would have led to a different equilibrium outcome if our agents had a different nature.

SON

		put orange in locker	*put nothing in locker*
	put apple in locker	3,3	1,4
FATHER			
	put nothing in locker	4,1	2,2

Figure 9–2. Fruit-exchange payoffs under the first assumption regarding human nature

For instance, if the father enjoyed sacrificing for his son and the son liked to be provided for by his father, then both the father and the son would like the outcome in which the son got both pieces of fruit best (4), the outcome in which the father got both pieces of fruit least (1), the outcome in which they exchange fruit second best (3), and the outcome in which they keep their original fruit next to last (2). In this case, Figure 9–3 would represent the utilities of the situation, and the equilibrium outcome would be the one circled, in which the son gets both pieces of fruit.

The upshot of all this is that one cannot discuss the properties of social or economic systems without making realistic assumptions about human nature. In our example, if for some reason we wanted the social outcome in which both the father and the son exchange their fruit, then it would be clear that under the set of rules we have defined and under either alternative definition of human nature, this outcome would not result. The only recourse is then either to change the rules or

SON

	put orange in locker	put nothing in locker
put apple **in locker**	3,3	4,4 <u>=</u>
put nothing **in locker**	1,1	2,2

FATHER

Figure 9–3. Fruit-exchange payoffs under the second assumption regarding human nature

change human nature, and obviously the former must be easier than the latter.

The origin and definition of human nature are, of course, complicated and controversial questions. Some observers, such as sociobiologist E. O. Wilson, think that much of our social behavior (or at least the parameters within which this behavior can vary) is genetically determined.[1] In this view, behavioral traits that yield behavior beneficial to the survival of the gene determining them increase the fitness of the human beings holding them and get transmitted from generation to generation with relatively greater frequency than those that do not, which are weeded out. In this view our current emotional makeup, degree of empathy for others, and sense of fairness are what they are for very specific functional, genetic purposes, just as the gills of fish exist for very specific purposes. For other observers, namely Marxists, the process is reversed. Humanity's mode of social and economic organization and its relationship to the means of production determine human nature. Consequently, each economic system creates the type of being whose nature is complementary to that mode of organization. Capitalism creates the bourgeoisie, socialism the new socialist man. In true dialectical fashion, these beings eventually destroy the stability of the system in which they function. Other scholars, particularly cultural anthropologists, view culture as the prime mover of human nature and view humanity as being socialized and molded by the culture in which it is raised.

Whatever view one wishes to take, the overwhelming fact is that any proposed economic or social system is bound to lead to outcomes different from those intended if the incentive system it employs is not consistent with the basic human nature of the agents who must participate in it. One need only look to the early American communal utopian experiments, such as Brook Farm and New Harmony, for examples of societies that failed by misperceiving the motives and basic nature of their participants.

HUMAN CULTURE AND SOCIOECONOMIC SYSTEMS

People evolve social institutions to help them solve a variety of recurrent everyday problems. These institutions define regularities in behavior that help social agents conduct their lives in an orderly way.[2] Like the convention of language, social institutions give structure to our everyday life.[3] They also fossilize our behavior and make it less flexible. For instance, Americans drive on the right hand side of the road and find adjusting to driving in Britain a harrowing experience. Old European gentlemen can find it hard to deal with young American feminists, since their urge to hold open doors for women or hold coats for them as they put them on is sometimes too great to control. Changes in social policies should be made with a realization that they will be more successful if they do not violate social regularities in behavior.

ECONOMIC FAIRNESS

For an economic system to survive, the outcome that it defines must be viewed as fair or justifiable by most of the agents in society. One of the most striking aspects of the American free enterprise system is the extent to which people, no matter how poor, feel that the rich are entitled to the incomes they earn, no matter how large. Instead of resenting the incomes of sports superstars or corporate executives, the population seems to turn these people into cultural heroes and idolize them. This fact is probably responsible for the great stability of American society and the rather weak demands historically for any radical income redistribution.

PRODUCTIVITY AND ECONOMIC SYSTEMS

Economic systems should be productive. That is their first and foremost requirement and the principal basis upon which they should be judged. The best measure of efficiency is the one used by economists—Pareto efficiency. By this measure, a societal organization of production is deemed inefficient if there exists another organization that is capable of producing more of every good, or at least more of some goods and no less of all others.

HOW THE FREE MARKET MEASURES UP

The system of free market economics in America generally measures up well to these criteria in the minds of most Americans. First, if we assume that human beings are primarily self-interested and concerned about their own well-being, then the free market system is particularly well suited to motivating them to be productive. In fact, a case could be made that the system would break down if people were anything but selfish and rational. Hence, if one assumes that human nature is as dismal as economists and free market advocates think, then the system of perfect competition certainly seems consistent with human nature.

With its emphasis on individualism and freedom of action, the free market system is particularly congenial to the American political ideology and cultural heritage of "rugged individualism," enterprise, and freedom. In fact, one important reason why people came to America in the eighteenth, nineteenth, and twentieth centuries was to be free to take their chances in the free market system. To this day Americans feel that a free enterprise system is a necessary condition for personal liberty and democracy. In four surveys taken in 1975, 1976, 1977, and 1979 by Cambridge Reports Inc., the following question was asked: "Some people say that a free market economy is necessary for personal liberty. Other people say the two aren't really related and we can be free and democratic in any kind of economy. Is a free market essential to freedom?" Majorities of 54 percent in 1975, 59 percent in 1976, 60 percent in 1977, and 59 percent in 1979 replied that a free market system was essential for freedom, 15–19 percent said it was not, while 25–27 percent were not sure. Hence, it is no wonder that the free market system has remained healthy in America, since a large majority of the population feels that tampering with it would mean a loss of their political freedom.[4]

One of the puzzles about the American free market system that must be resolved is why people living under it tend to think that the outcomes it defines are fair. For instance, one would at least think that those people who do relatively poorly in the market process (i.e., the lowest 20 percent of the income distribution) would resent the incomes earned by the top 5 percent of income earners. Yet, remarkably, this does not seem to be the case.

Lipset and Schneider report on a 1977 poll of Yankelovich in which the public rejected the proposition "The free enterprise system benefits the few" by a margin of 52 percent to 16 percent. Further, in a Harris poll taken in that same year in which 1,625 people were asked to comment on the proposition "The business system if regulated equitably by the Federal government can operate equitably for the vast majority of the people in this country," 60 percent agreed, 17 percent disagreed, and 23 percent were not sure. In 1976 a similar question yielded 72-percent agreement, 14-percent disagreement and 14-percent uncertainty. Clearly the American public perceives the system either as fair or as capable of being made fair without major dislocations.

This belief in the equity of the free market system may stem from the fact that Americans tend to feel that income cannot be fundamentally redistributed without ruining the freedoms and incentives the free market system grants. All free market advocates, even those that do relatively poorly, feel that they would lose more by the destruction of the free market system than they would gain from any income transfer they might receive. Support for this view can be seen in a 1977 Harris poll, which shows that when people were presented with the statement, "For all of its faults the American economic system still provides our people with the highest living standards in the world," 88 percent agreed, 8 percent disagreed, and 4 percent were not sure. Furthermore, in a 1974 Roper poll in which people were asked which of 13 national characteristics they considered "major causes of United States greatness," 60 percent chose the free enterprise system.

With such views of the fairness of the free market system, it is no surprise that there has never been more than superficial movements in the United States toward any type of income redistribution. Arguments about income inequality seem to fall on deaf ears, even when those ears belong to the poor.

Finally, the American free market has been extraordinarily productive. No statistics need be presented to demonstrate the fact that no country on earth has achieved the economic growth and performance that the United States has—a fact that is not surprising since the *raison d'être* of free market systems is efficiency and productivity. More important for the stability of the free market system is the fact that Americans believe that their productivity is a result of the free market system they live in. For instance, in 1977 a Harris poll found that 60 percent of the population agreed with the statement "The American free enterprise system is the most efficient economically the world has ever known," while only 20 percent disagreed. By a margin of 51 percent to 28 percent, Americans believed that "If left alone, except for essential federal regulations, the free enterprise system can find ways to solve such problems as inflation and unemployment."

In summation, the American free enterprise system easily satisfies the four criteria specified for a stable economic system. Its productivity is unquestionable; it presents a system of economic organization that fits easily into our political and cultural heritage; it is consistent with a distasteful but probably accurate view of human nature; and it is perceived as fair. Furthermore, people seem to think that they have much to lose from termination of the free enterprise system in America. With these attributes it is no surprise that free enterprise is alive and well in the United States.

NOTES

1. E. O. Wilson, *Sociobiology: The New Synthesis,* Cambridge, MA: Harvard University Press, 1975.
2. Andrew Schotter, *The Economic Theory of Social Institutions,* New York: Cambridge University Press, 1981.
3. David Lewis, *Convention,* Cambridge, MA: Harvard University Press, 1969.
4. All of the references to surveys in this chapter can be found in a new and interesting book by Seymour Lipset and William Schneider, *The Confidence Gap: Business, Labor and Government in the Public Mind,* New York: Macmillan, 1983.

10

Conclusion

As I stated in the preface, my aim has been to make the reader more skeptical of the free market solution to social problems by presenting a set of immanent criticisms of the free market argument. In this process several ironies came to light. First, we saw how individual rationality, the very cornerstone of the competitive process, can cause markets to fail. In instance after instance, we saw situations (markets with asymmetric information, public goods, externalities, etc.) in which Adam Smith's invisible hand pushed economic agents beyond the point of efficiency and into mutual self-destruction. Further, using the prisoner's dilemma game as an example, we saw how individually rational behavior can determine social outcomes that are worse for *all* agents in an economy than coordinated social behavior.

Next, we saw in our discussion of educational vouchers and the minimum wage that markets with no *apparent* externalities may be filled with them. For instance, when one takes the rational actions of corner dwellers into account, the possible failure of competitive labor markets to determine more than subsistence wages transforms supposedly externality-free markets into markets that generate distasteful externalities such as crime. Accepting the free market form of eco-

163

nomic organization has its price. If, as Adam Smith felt, free markets work because individual agents are rational and self-interested, then we cannot expect socially minded or altruistic behavior to emerge when they fail. If incentives exist to report false preferences for public goods, then we can expect people to do so. If, in the absence of property rights, it pays to pollute a lake, then rational self-interested agents will pollute. If crime is a possible rational response to poverty wages, we can expect crime to arise. This is not to say that when all the costs and benefits are weighed it would not be wise to opt for the free market system of economic organization. However, it must be recognized that doing so involves costs, and that in certain circumstances these costs may be too high to be outweighed by the benefits of the free market.

Further, the types of goods we want allocated by the free market may be quite different from the types of goods we want allocated by non-market mechanisms. For instance, BMWs seem to be an appropriate good to allocate using markets. Kidney or heart operations seem less appropriate, since the right to life should be independent of whether one can afford a particular operation.[1]

In short, we must not be doctrinaire in our advocacy of free market solutions to all of our social and economic problems. When appropriate, the market should be used, but when other, non-market institutions seem more reasonable or when markets can be expected to fail, then we must search for, design, and test other allocating mechanisms to replace the market. The search for these mechanisms will be an important item on the research agenda of economists in the years to come.

NOTE

1. Guido Calabresi and Philip Bobbitt, *Tragic Choices*, New York: W. W. Norton, 1978.

Glossary

Blame-free justice: a concept of justice whereby an outcome of a social institution in a society is justifiable if no social agent in the society can blame any other agent for the actions taken in defining that outcome.

Corner solutions: a solution to a mathematical maximization problem in which some of the variables determined by the maximization take on a zero value.

Efficiency-equity tradeoff assumption: the assumption that unless an individualistic social ethic is used to define the equity of social outcomes, there is likely to be an unfortunate tradeoff between the ethic used and the efficiency of the outcomes determined by the social institutions.

Expected-utility hypothesis: a hypothesis about the way rational people go about making decisions in situations characterized by uncertainty. It claims that people first define utility numbers and place them on the monetary values involved in their decisions. Then, given the probabilities defined over the uncertain variables in the situation, these people make the decision that maximizes their expected utility.

Externalities: costs or benefits that one social agent confers on another through the act of consuming or producing. Since these costs or benefits are external to the agent conferring them, they are not taken into account when that agent decides how intensively he wants to engage in a particular act.

Immanent criticism: a criticism of a theory that does not challenge that theory's assumptions but rather accepts them and tries to show that they are either inconsistent or lead to wrong or undesirable conclusions.

Individualism: a political philosophy that looks to the individual as the ultimate reservoir for all rights and obligations in society. From this philosophy follows the normative belief that all social decisions ought to be mere reflections of individual preferences and that no outside authority should have the right to impose his preferences on society.

Invisible-hand laissez-faire faith assumption: an assumption, coming originally from Adam Smith's classic *The Wealth of Nations*, that states that if individuals are left alone and allowed to contract voluntarily, the welfare of society will be enhanced. Any intervention in this process is bound to make things worse.

Markets with asymmetric information: markets in which one side of the market is better informed about the characteristics of the products being sold than is the other side.

Paretian calculation: one of several types of calculations that can be used to make social decisions. It dictates that decision A is better than decision B if, when comparing the happiness of all agents in society under these two alternative decisions, *all* people are better off or happier if decision A is taken rather than decision B.

Process-oriented argument: an argument that in judging the ethical properties of outcomes defined by social institutions one must look only at the properties of the process determining these outcomes (i.e., the rules of the game) and not at the properties of the end-states of these processes (i.e., the income distributions they define). If the process determining a particular set of outcomes is "fair," then those outcomes must be "fair," no matter how unequal they may appear.

Public good: a good whose use cannot be excluded once the good is created. In addition, one person's consumption of the good does not diminish the amount of the good available for anyone else. Public defense is a classic example of a public good.

Rational expectations: expectations made by economic agents using the relevant theory of their given situation to form those expectations.

Theory of games: the theory, developed by John Von Neumann and Oskar Morgenstern in *The Theory of Games and Economic Behavior,* that studies the strategic interdependence among social agents. This theory concentrates on those situations in which one agent's utility depends not only upon the actions that he takes in a particular social situation but also on the actions taken by the other agents in that situation.

Utilitarian calculation: one of several types of calculations that can be used to make social decisions. The decision as to whether to build a road through a bird sanctuary or a suburban neighborhood discussed on page 3 is a utilitarian calculation. A person using a utilitarian calculation makes that decision with the greatest net social benefits (social benefits minus social costs). Many times in economics, this boils down to making the social decision that maximizes the difference between the amount of money society is willing to pay for a particular decision (the consumer's willingness to pay) and the amount of money that will have to be sacrificed to make it (the decision's social cost).

Bibliography

Akerlof, George, "The Market for Lemons: Quality, Uncertainty and Market Mechanism," *Quarterly Journal of Economics*, August 1970, pp. 488–500.

Alchian, Armen, A., "Uncertainty, Evolution and Economic Theory," *Journal of Political Economy*, June 1950, 58(3), pp. 211–221.

Allais, M., "Le Comportement de l'Homme Rational Devant le Risque: Critiques de Postulates et Axioms de l'Ecole Americaine," *Econometrica*, October 1953, 21(4), pp. 503–546.

Arrow, Kenneth, *Individual Choice and Social Value*, 2nd edition, New York; Wiley, 1963.

Arrow, Kenneth, and Frank Hahn, *General Competitive Analysis*, San Francisco: Holden Day, 1970.

Baumol, William, *Welfare Economics and the Theory of the State*, London: Longmans Green, 1952.

Baxter, William F., *People or Penguins: The Case for Optimal Pollution*, New York: Columbia University Press, 1974.

Bentham, Jeremy, *Principles of Morals and Legislation*, Oxford: Wilfred Hamson, 1948.

Berman, S. M., and Andrew Schotter, "When Is the Incentive Problem Real?" *Games, Economic Dynamics, and Time Series Analysis*, 1982.

Bohm, P., "Estimating Demand for Public Goods: An Experiment," *European Economic Review*, Vol. 3, 1982, pp. 111–130.

Buchanan, James, "A Contractarian Paradism for Applying Economic Theory," *American Economic Review*, 65(2) May 1975, pp. 225–231.

Buchanan, James, and Geoffrey Brennan, *The Power to Tax*, Cambridge, England: Cambridge University Press, 1980.

Bull, C., A. Schotter and K. Weigelt, "Asymmetric Tournaments, Equal Opportunity Laws and Affirmative Action: Some Experimental Results." C. V. Starr Center for Applied Economics, Research Report 8733, 1987a.

——, ——, and ——, "Tournaments and Piece Rate: An Experimental Study," *Journal of Political Economy*, Vol. 95, Feb. 1987b, pp. 1–33.

Calabresi, Guido and Philip Bobbit, *Tragic Choices*, New York: W. W. Norton, 1978.

Clarke, Edward, "Multipart Pricing of Public Goods," *Public Choice*, 11, pp. 17–33.

Coase, Ronald, "The Problem of Special Cost," *Journal of Law and Economics*, 3, 1960, pp. 1–44.

Condorcet, Marquise de, "Essai sur l'application de l'analyse à la probabilité des decisions rendues à la pluralets de voix," Paris, 1785.

Cooter, Robert, and Kornhauser, Lewis, "Can Litigation Improve the Law Without the Help of Judges?" *Journal of Legal Studies*, 9, January 1980, pp. 139–165.

Debreu, Gerald, *The Theory of Value*, New York: Wiley, 1959.

Economic Report of the President, Government Printing Office, Washington, D.C., 1982.

Foley, Duncan, "Resource Allocation and the Public Sector," *Yale Economic Essays*, Spring 1967.

Friedman, Milton, *Capitalism and Freedom*, Chicago: Chicago University Press, 1962.

Frydman, Roman, "Towards an Understanding of Market Processes: Individual Expectations, Learning and Convergence to Rational Expectations Equilibrium," *American Economic Review*, 72(4), September 1982, pp. 652–668.

——, Gerald O'Driscoll, and Andrew Schotter, "Rational Expectations of Government Policy: An Application of Newcomb's Problem," *Southern Journal of Economics*, 42(2), October 1982, pp. 311–319.

Gardner, Martin, "Mathematical Games," *Scientific American*, July 1973, pp. 104–108.

Green, Jerry, and Jean Jacques Laffont, *Incentives in Public Decision Making*, Amsterdam: North Holland, 1979.

Grether, David, and Charles Plott, "Economic Theory of Choice and the Preference Reversal Phenomenon," *American Economic Review*, 69(4), September 1979, pp. 623–638.

Grossman, Sanford J., "On the Efficiency of Competitive Stock Markets Where Traders Have Diverse Information," *Journal of Finance*, May 1976, pp. 573–585.

——, "The Existence of Futures Markets, Noisy Rational Expectations, and Informational Externalities," *Review of Economic Studies*, October 1977, pp. 431–449.

Grossman, Sanford J., and Joseph E. Stiglitz, "Information and Competitive Price Systems," *American Economic Review*, May 1976, pp. 246–253.

Groves, Theodore, "Incentives in Teams," *Econometrica*, 41, July 1973, pp. 617–631.

Hardin, R., "Collective Action as an Agreeable n-Prisoner's Dilemma," *Behavioral Science*, 16, September 1971, pp. 472–481.

Hare, R. M., *Freedom and Reason*, Oxford: Oxford University Press, 1963.

Harrison, Bennet, "Education and Unemployment in the Urban Ghetto," *American Economic Review*, 62(5), 1972, pp. 796–812.

Harrod, Roy, "Utilitarianism Revised," *Mind*, 45, 1936, pp. 137–156.

Hayek, F. A., "Economics and Knowledge," *Economica*, 4, 1937, pp. 33–54.

——, *Individualism and Economic Order*, Chicago: University of Chicago Press, 1948.

——, *Law, Legislation and Liberty*, Chicago: University of Chicago Press, 1976.

Hoffman, E., and M. Spitzer, "Entitlements, Rights and Fairness: An Experimental Examination of Subject's Concepts of Distribution Justice," *Journal of Legal Studies*, Vol. 14, November 2 1985, pp. 259–297.

——, and ——, "The Coase Theorem: Some Experimental Tests," *Journal of Law and Economics*, Vol. 25, 1982, pp. 93–98.

Hume, David, *A Treatise on Human Nature*, Oxford: Oxford University Press, 1896.

Isaac, M., K. McCue and C. Plott, "Public Goods Provision in an Experimental Environment," *Journal of Public Economics*, Vol 26, 1985, pp. 51–74.

Jevons, William, *The Theory of Political Economy*, Middlesex, England: Penguin, 1970.

Johansen, L., "The Theory of Public Goods Misplaced Emphasis," *Journal of Public Economics*, Vol. 7, 1977, pp. 149–152.

Kahneman, D., and A. Tversky, "Prospect Theory: An Analysis of Decision Under Risk," *Econometrica*, 47, 1979, pp. 263–291.

Kaldor, N., "Welfare Propositions of Economics and Interpersonal Comparisons of Utility," *Economic Journal*, 49, 1939, pp. 549–552.

Kydland, Finne, and Edward Prescott, "Rules Rather Than Discretion: The Inconsistency of Optimal Plans," *Journal of Political Economy*, June 1977, pp. 473–491.

Lerner, Abba, *The Economics of Control*, New York: Macmillan, 1944.

Levitan, Sar, and Richard Belous, *More Than Subsistence: Minimum Wage for the Working Poor*, Baltimore: Johns Hopkins University Press, 1979.

Lewis, David, *Convention*, Cambridge, MA: Harvard University Press, 1969.

Liebenstein, Harvey, "Bandwagon, Snob and Veblen Effects in the Theory of Consumers Demand," *Quarterly Journal of Economics*, 65, 1950, pp. 183–207.

——, "Allocative vs. X-Efficiency," *American Economic Review*, Vol. 56, June 1966, pp. 392–415.

Lipset, Seymour, and William Schneider, *The Confidence Gap: Business, Labor and Government in the Public Mind*, New York: Macmillan, 1983.

Locke, John, *Two Treatises of Government*, Cambridge, England: Cambridge University Press, 1960, pp. 305–306.

Lucas, Robert E., Jr., "Some International Evidence on Output-Inflation Tradeoffs," *American Economic Review*, June 1973, pp. 326–334.

Margolis, Howard, *Selfishness, Altruism and Rationality: A Theory of Social Choice*, New York: Cambridge University Press, 1982.

Marwell, G. and R. Ames, "Economists Free Ride, Does Anyone Else? Experiments on the Provision of Public Goods," *Journal of Public Economics*, Vol. 15, 1981, pp. 295–310.

Musgrave, Richard, *The Theory of Public Finance*, New York: McGraw-Hill, 1959.

Muth, John F., "Rational Expectations and the Theory of Price Movement," *Econometrica*, July 1961, pp. 315–335.

Nash, George, *The Conservative Intellectual Movement in America Since 1945*, New York: Masic Books, 1976.

Nash, John, "The Bargaining Problem," *Econometrica*, 18, 1950, pp. 155–162.

Nozick, Robert, *Anarchy, State and Utopia* New York: Basic Books, 1976.

——, "Summary of Readers' Responses," *Scientific American*, March 1974.

O'Driscoll, Gerald, *Economics As a Coordinating Problem*, Kansas City: Sheed, Andres and MacNeel, 1977.

Pascale, Richard Tanner, and Anthony Athos, *Art of Japanese Management*, New York: Simon and Schuster, 1981.

Phelps, Edmund S., "Obstacles to Curtailing Inflation," in *Essays in Post Keynesian Inflation*, James H. Gapinski and Charles E. Rockwood, eds., Cambridge, MA: Ballinger, 1979.

Pitchik, Carolyn, and Andrew Schotter, Internal and External Regulation of Markets with Asymmetric Information," unpublished paper at NYU, second revision, April 1983.

——, and ——, "Regulating Markets with Asymmetric Information: An Experimental Study." C. V. Starr Center Research Report, 1985.

Plott, C. and L. Wilde, "Professional Diagnosis vs. Self Diagnosis: An Experimental Examination of Some Special Features of Markets with Uncertainty," *Research in Experimental Economics*, Vol. 2, ed. Vernon Smith, Greenwich Connecticut, JAI Press, 1982.

Posner, Richard, *The Economic Analysis of the Law*, Boston: Little Brown and Company, 1972.

——, *The Economics of Justic*, Cambridge, MA: Harvard University Press, 1981.

Rawls, John, *A Theory of Justice*, Cambridge, MA: Harvard University Press, 1971.

"Resurgence of Sweatshops in New York," *New York Times*, 26 February 1981.

Roth, A., "Laboratory Experimentation in Economics: A Methodological Overview," *The Economic Journal*, Vol. 98(393), December 1988, pp. 994–1032.

Rothschild, Michael, and Joseph Stiglitz, "Equilibrium in Competitive Insurance Markets: An Essay on the Economics of Imperfect Competition," *Quarterly Journal of Economics*, 90(4), 1976, pp. 629–649.

Sargent, Thomas, J. and Wallace, Neil, *Rational Expectations and the Theory of Economic Policy: Studies in Monetary Economics*, Minneapolis: Federal Reserve Bank of Minneapolis Research Department, 1975.

Schneider, F. and W. Pommerehne, "Free Riding and Collective Action: An Experiment in Public Microeconomics," *Quarterly Journal of Economics*, Vol. 116, 1981, pp. 689–704.

Schoemaker, Paul, "The Expected Utility Model: Its Variant Purposes, Evidence and Limitations," *Journal of Economic Literature*, 201(2), June 1982, pp. 529–563.

Schotter, Andrew, *The Economic Theory of Social Institutions*, New York: Cambridge University Press, 1981.

Schotter, A. and K. Weigelt, "The Benefits of Equal Opportunity," *Business and Society Review*, Spring 1988, pp. 45–48.

Sen, Amartya, *Collective Choice and Social Welfare*, San Francisco: Holden Day, 1970.

Shapley, Lloyd, "A Value for n-Person Games," *Contributions to the Theory of Games* II, Annals of Mathematics Studies, 28, Princeton, NJ: Princeton University Press, 1953.

Simon, Herbert A., "Rational Decision Making in Business Organizations," *American Economic Review*, 69, September 1979, pp. 496–523.

Simon, William, *A Time for Truth*, New York: McGraw-Hill, 1978.

Smart, J. J. C and Bernard Williams, *Utilitarianism: For and Against*, Cambridge, England: Cambridge University Press, 1975.

Smith, Adam, *Theory of Moral Sentiments*, Oxford, Clarendon Press, 1976.

——, *The Wealth of Nations*, Indianapolis: Liberty Classics, 1981.

Sowell, Thomas, *Knowledge and Decisions*, New York: Basic Books, 1981.

Thaler, Richard, "Towards a Positive Theory of Consumer Choice," *Journal of Economic Behavior and Organization*, 1, 1981, pp. 39–60.

Tideman, Nicholas and Gordon Tullock, "A New and Superior Process for Making Social Choices," *Journal of Political Economy*, 84, 1976, pp. 1145–1159.

Varian, Hal, "Equity, Envy and Efficiency," *Journal of Economic Theory*, 9, 1974, pp. 1–23.

Vickerey, William, "Counter Speculation, Auctions and Competitive Sealed Tenders," *Journal of Finance*, 16, pp. 8–37.

Wilson, Charles, "Model of Insurance Markets with Incomplete Information," *Journal of Economic Theory*, 16(2), October 1977, pp. 167–207.

Wilson, E. O., *Sociobiology: The New Synthesis*, Cambridge, MA: Harvard University Press, 1975.

Zucker, Alfred, "Minimum Wages and the Long Run Demand for Low Wage Labor," *Quarterly Journal of Economics*, May 1973, pp. 267–277.

Index